To
TAKE OFF
The
COVER

To TAKE OFF *The* COVER

Revealing the Identity of the Antichrist

TIMOTHY WIKSTROM

XULON PRESS

Xulon Press
2301 Lucien Way #415
Maitland, FL 32751
407.339.4217
www.xulonpress.com

Unless otherwise indicated, Scripture quotations taken from the King James Version (KJV)–*public domain.*

Printed in the United States of America.

Paperback ISBN-13: 978-1-6628-0002-3
eBook ISBN-13: 978-1-6628-0003-0

To Andrew and Abby. . . I love you so much.

You make me incredibly happy, and I'm so proud to be your Dad. Please always know and don't ever Forget that in this life, the only person that you need is The Heavenly Father. He's the One who loves You with a perfect love and always has your best interest no Matter what the circumstances look like.

With Him you can accomplish anything; you can defeat any giant, Walk through every valley, and triumph over All fiery trials.

"…He that heareth, let him hear; and He that forbeareth, let him forbear…"

[King James Version, Ezekiel 3:27]

TABLE OF CONTENTS

INTRODUCTION

WHO DOESN'T LOVE A GOOD MYSTERY? I BELIEVE I can say that almost everyone enjoys a good old-fashioned, "Who done it?" Whether it's a book or a movie that causes us to so anxiously try and figure out who the killer is, we all enjoy the thrill and, yes, even the surprise at the end when we learn who it was that had us so tied up in knots and caused us to guess in error so many times. Well, this book revolves around a very old and highly mysterious question that has remained unanswerable until now; and that question is, "Who is the antichrist?"

For approximately 2000 years, people of all kinds have wondered and have desperately tried to figure out just who is this man that will staunchly oppose God, The Father and His Son, Jesus Christ; and they also have wondered who is this man that Satan, God's original enemy since the beginning of time, will use in such an incredible but extremely effective way. Well, I think it would be even fair to say that we all have heard several different names pop up when the topic of "Who is The Antichrist?" arose, names like Ronald Reagan, Nero, and the recent, popular guess, Barack Obama; but thank God for His holy word and the fact that He is still willing to reveal hidden and special meanings in His word to His children, because that's exactly how I found out the identity of the antichrist:

> "…Blessed be the name of God for
> Ever and ever: for wisdom and
> Might are his: And he changeth
> The times and the seasons: he
> Removeth kings: he giveth wisdom
> Unto the wise, and knowledge to
> Them that know understanding:
> He revealeth the deep and secret
> Things…"
> Daniel 2: 20-23

So, since I, too, love a good mystery, and because the mystery surrounding the identity of the antichrist has been so great, I have decided to reveal who he is by giving five major clues, clues all given to me by the holy Father

Himself and clues all taken directly from his divine word. Along with the five major clues, other extremely relative and important revelations concerning the identity of the antichrist will also be included, and they, too, further prove and even totally cement the irrefutable fact of the antichrist really being who the holy word says that he, in fact, is. Please also note that throughout this book you will no doubt discover amazing and awesome truths of the biblical and historical nature that will most likely take your breath away or even cause you to exclaim quite loudly; that's ok. You certainly will not be the first person to do so, and you will definitely not be the last. These awesome truths, by the way, I've chosen to personally call them, "juicy tidbits;" again, they will astonish you.

Also, I have decided to keep the evidence of scripture to a maximum of three supporting references in some places only because of the amount of evidence sometimes can quite honestly be both staggering and overwhelming; my intent was never to achieve overkill in this area.

Now, in order to capture the full effect of this book's fantastic mystery as well as all the wonderful and unforgettable feelings that accompany it, feelings of anticipation, thrill, and pure astonishment, I *strongly* recommend that you do not peek, look ahead, or skip pages; trust me, if you do, you will be shortchanging yourself and miss out on a terrific blessing. The simple truth of the matter is this: This awesome book is designed to give you a very enjoyable and exciting ride, one that you will *never* forget. So, as I said, to experience the full effect of the wonderful and gripping mystery of this book, I highly recommend that you read the entirety of this book and do so page by page and word for word.

Lastly, please understand that the only reason why I'm able to positively identify and exclusively reveal to you who the antichrist actually is, is because of my holy Father revealing him to me; that's right; that's the *only* reason why; and He did that, for the most part, through His holy word. Therefore, please understand that all the incredible proof that I will reveal in this amazing book, including the five clues, comes not from me in any way, shape, or form. *All* of the evidence – all of it – that you are about to read concerning the unquestionable identity of the antichrist comes from God and God alone.

So, now that we've addressed all the formal issues, are you ready to try and solve the mystery that has been on-going and exhaustively debated for some 2000 years, the mystery that has continually escaped the guesses of countless human beings and has also been completely unsolvable, the mystery that could easily be stated as one of the greatest ever in the history of mankind? Are you? Are you up for the challenge? Alright, your incredible mystery starts now.

The Importance of Biblical Names

BIBLICAL NAMES ARE EXTREMELY IMPORTANT. If I were to list every instance in God's holy word where a person, place, or thing – that's right, even an object – had a name that had a very specific meaning attributed to that person, place, or thing, this book would have so many pages and be so incredibly thick that you would be reading until your 80 years old; well, hold that thought. What I mean to say is that you would be reading until you're 80 years old if you are now in, say, your twenties. *That's* how much The Holy Bible is filled with instances where a name is much more than just a name.

The importance of names in God's word, however, doesn't just stop there; no, it certainly doesn't. Symbolism can often be seen in the names. That's right, symbolism. Now, I personally have not inspected every single name in The

Holy Bible, but the people, places, and things that I do know that actually have symbolism associated with their names are, indeed, many and are scattered throughout. I must say: It truly is amazing how God's word really is alive, and how unless He opens our eyes and reveals the hidden meanings as well as the symbolic nature, we are not only blind, we're certainly a stick stuck in the mud.

What I'd like to do now is give you a few pieces of evidence to prove to you that names of a person, place, or thing in God's word are actually very deep in nature and contain much insight; and whether it was God Himself giving the name or just another human being, names in His word are extremely meaningful and of great importance. Here, now, are the three supporting references via a person:

- Samson was blessed with tremendous, supernatural strength. Unfortunately for him, however, he met a lady named delilah who made a monetary bribe with his enemies, and the end result was not good. Samson eventually became weak like a normal man and lost all of his supernatural strength. Now, check

this out: The actual meaning of Delilah's
name means, "languishing;"[1] yep, that's
right; that's what her name means, and
I think it's easy to see that all of Samson's
Supernatural strength was sapped or, shall
We say, *languished* through Delilah. By
The way, you can read this sad but true
Part of their personal story in the Book of
Judges, Chapter 6, verses 15-19.
The next scriptural reference regarding a person:

- "And the angel said unto her, Fear not,
  Mary: for thou hast found favour with
  God. And, behold, thou shalt conceive
  In they womb, and bring forth a son, and
  Shalt call his name JESUS."
  Luke 1: 30-31

---

[1] Taken from *THE NEW STRONG'S EXHAUSTIVE CONCORDANCE OF THE BIBLE* by Strong, James, LL.D., S.T.D., 32

Among other things, the name, "Jesus" actual Hebraic meaning is "Jehovah saved."[2] Well, after all, He is the Savior of the world; here, you see for yourself:

> "Be it known unto you all, and to all
> The people of Israel, that by the name
> Crucified, whom God raised from the
> Dead … Neither is there salvation in
> Any other: for there is none other
> Name under Heaven given among
> Men, whereby we must be saved."
> Acts 4: 10, 12
> A place:

- "And Jacob was left alone; and there
  Wrestled a man with him until the breaking
  Of the day. And when he saw that he
  Prevailed not against him, he touched the
  Hollow of his thigh; and the hollow of
  Jacob's thigh was out of joint, as he
  Wrestled with him. And he said, Let me
  Go, for the day breaketh. And he said, I
  Will not let thee go, except thou bless me.

---

[2] Ibid., 61

And he said unto him, What is they name?
And he said, Jacob. And he said, Thy
Name shall be called no more Jacob, but
Israel: for as a prince hast thou power
With God and with men, and hast pre-
Vailed. And Jacob asked him, and said,
Tell me, I pray thee, thy name. And he
Said, Wherefore is it that thou dost ask
After my name? And he blessed him
There. And Jacob called the name of the
Place Peniel: for I have seen God face
To face, and my life is preserved."
Genesis 32: 24-30

The word, "Peniel" means "face of God."[3]
The next scriptural reference:

- "And David was displeased, because the
Lord had made a breach upon Uzza:
Wherefore that place is called Perez-uzza
To this day."
1 Chronicles 13: 11

---

[3] Ibid., 115

The word, "Perez-uzza" means "break of Uzza."[4]
A thing:

- After Gideon saw the angel of the Lord
  Face to face, "…the Lord said unto him,
  Peace be unto thee: fear not: thou
  Shalt not die. Then Gideon built an altar
  There unto the Lord, and called it
  Jehovah-shalom…"
  Judges 6: 23-24

The meaning of Jehovah-shalom is "Jehovah is peace."[5]

So, as you can see, names of people, places, and even things in God's word whether prophetic in nature or not, are, indeed, extremely important, and they also give the reader more insight as well as a better, overall understanding. What's also interesting (that is if you really are a child of God, have repented of your sins, and have placed your trust in the Lord Jesus as your personal Savior.) is that one day you will actually receive a new name from

---

[4] Ibid., 117

[5] Ibid., 54

God Himself. Yep, I kid you not; you sure will, and here's the proof:

> "And the Gentiles shall see thy
> Righteousness, and all kinds thy
> Glory; and thou shalt be called
> By a new name, which the mouth
> Of the Lord shall name."
> Isaiah 62: 2
> "To him that overcometh will I give
> To eat of the hidden manna, and
> Will give him a white stone, and
> In the stone a new name written,
> Which no man knoweth saving he
> that receiveth it."
> Revelation 2: 17

See, as you just witnessed for yourself, our new name that we will receive from God will no doubt be representative of the type of person we are, the personality that we have, and the character that we possess.

Alright, next up: The first clue, Clue #1: Pride is His Best Friend

Pride is His Best Friend

Pride and the antichrist go hand in hand; they are one and the same; they are joined at the hip; they are each other's best friend. The antichrist is evil. No doubt he is wicked, but probably the single most appropriate attribute God's word uses to define the antichrist is none other than pride.

In many of the holy scriptures, pride can readily be seen characterizing the antichrist; yep, it sure can. However, The Holy Bible doesn't just address the antichrist alone by his official title. No, it certainly does not. Actually, God's word has many different names it uses to address him, and many, in fact, all point to, as we just learned in the previous chapter of this book, his character, personality and the type of actions that will emerge and be clearly seen as a result from the type of person that he is, with pride, of course, being the most dominant and most spoken characteristic used in the holy scriptures to perfectly describe the antichrist.

For example, "the lofty," "most proud," "the pride of Assyria," "the terrible," "the man of sin," "the mighty man," "the son of perdition," "the mean man," "the bough," "the haughty," and "the king," are just some of the names that God uses to address that Lofty Lunatic of Lucifer, and that really shouldn't surprise you, because the antichrist's boss, Satan, is also all too familiar with pride himself. In fact, in his own selfish and sinister folly, he unwisely allowed pride to lift up and corrupt his heart instead of allowing God to lovingly touch it; here, now, is the proof:

> "Thine heart was lifted up
> Because of thy beauty, thou
> Hast corrupted thy wisdom by
> Reason of thy brightness..."
> Ezekiel 28: 17

The following scriptures are used by The Holy Bible to showcase the antichrist's affinity for pride and also, at the same time, they definitely help clue us in on the unmistakable identity of the antichrist:

"Behold, I am against thee, O thou most
Proud [the antichrist], saith the Lord
God of hosts: for thy day is come, the
Time that I will visit thee. And the most
Proud [the antichrist] shall stumble and
Fall and none shall raise him up…"
Jeremiah 50: 31-32

"and, behold, in this horn [the antichrist]
Were eyes like the eyes of man, and a
Mouth speaking great things."
Daniel 7: 8

"I beheld then because of the voice of the
Great words which the horn [the
antichrist] spake."
Daniel 7: 11

"even of that horn [the antichrist] that
Had eyes, and a mouth that spake
Very great things…"
Daniel 7: 20

"and he [the antichrist] shall speak

Great words against the Most High…"
Daniel 7: 25

"Yea, he [the antichrist] magnified
Himself even to the prince of the
host…"
Daniel 8: 11

"and he [the antichrist] shall magnify
Himself in his heart…"
Daniel 8: 25

"And the king [the antichrist] shall do
According to his will; and he shall exalt
Himself, and magnify himself above
Every god, and shall speak marvelous
Things against the God of gods…for he
Shall magnify himself above all."
Daniel 11: 36-37

"…and the pride of Assyria [the antichrist]
Shall be brought down…"
Zechariah 10: 11

"that man of sin [the antichrist]

Revealed, the son of perdition [the
Antichrist]; Who opposeth and ex-
Alteth himself above all that is called
God, or that is worshipped; so that he
As God sitteth in the temple as God,
Shewing himself that he is God."
2 Thessalonians 2: 3-4

"And there was given unto him [the
Antichrist] a mouth speaking great
Things and blasphemies…"
Revelation 13: 5

"And the mean man [the antichrist]
Shall be brought down, and the mighty
Man [the antichrist] shall be humbled,
And the eyes of the lofty [the antichrist]
Shall be humbled."
Isaiah 5: 15

Ok, the three, following passages also speak of that
Lofty Lunatic of Lucifer, and afterwards Pastor Jimmy
Swaggart will certainly bless us with some wonderful and
very insightful commentary. Here, now, are the passages:

"The lofty looks of man [the antichrist]
Shall be humbled, and the haughtiness
Of men shall be bowed down, and the
Lord alone shall be exalted in that day.
For the day of the Lord of hosts shall be
Upon every one that is proud and lofty,
And upon every one that is lifted up; and
He shall be brought low…And the loftiness
Of man [the antichrist] shall be bowed
Down, and the haughtiness of men
Shall be laid low; and the Lord alone
Shall be exalted in that day."
Isaiah 2: 11-12; 17

"Behold, the Lord, the Lord of hosts,
Shall lop the bough [the antichrist]
With terror; and the high ones of
Stature shall be hewn down, and
The haughty [the antichrist] shall
Be humbled."
Isaiah 10: 33

"And I [God] will punish the world for
Their evil, and the wicked for their
Iniquity; and I will cause the arrogancy

> Of the proud [the antichrist] to cease,
> And will lay low the haughtiness of the
> Terrible [the antichrist]."
> Isaiah 13: 11

Pastor Swaggart now wonderfully elaborates on the first passage:

"In that day" refers to the Second Advent.
The "man with the lofty looks" is the Antichrist."[6]
"the very nature of the Antichrist and all who follow him will be proud and lofty"[7]
"This Passage is very similar to verse 11, and is so intended by the Holy Spirit.
The very nature of the Antichrist and His followers will be "pride." But he
And all his minions "shall be made low."[8]
Pastor Swaggart on the second passage:
"The "haughty" speaks of the Antichrist
And how he will be "humbled" by the

---

[6] Jimmy Swaggart, *"The Expositor's Study Bible"* (Baton Rouge: Jimmy Swaggart Ministries, 2010), 1104

[7] Ibid, 1104

[8] Ibid, 1105

Lord Jesus Christ."[9]
Pastor Swaggart once more on the last passage of scripture:
"The proud" and "the terrible" refer to
The Antichrist in particular and to all
His followers in general."[10]

So, see, as you have just witnessed, the antichrist will certainly be dominated by pride. In fact, he'll be full of it. Oh, wait, that didn't sound too good; but then again, I don't think that last statement would be so unfair or even somewhat incorrect to say; no, I certainly don't. I mean, seriously, since pride *is* his best friend, then humility must be his enemy or surely something he definitely has no interest in attaining. Why do I say that? Well, simply because, this man – the antichrist – will be so lofty, so self-absorbed, so arrogant and haughty, he will make *all* the narcissists that have ever lived *in the entire history of mankind* look like Moses, a man known for his godly meekness:

> "(Now the man Moses was very meek,
> Above all men that were upon the face

---

[9] Ibid, 1120

[10] Ibid, 1123

Of the earth.)"
Numbers 12: 3

Now, I must say that's one of the personal traits that I definitely need my life to be defined by: meekness.

Alright, with that Clue #1: Pride is His Best Friend has now been totally presented and is now complete. Next up: Clue #2: His Deadly Wound. Ooohh, you're so going to love that clue! That clue is totally amazing and fascinating!

His Deadly Wound

This piece of information regarding the antichrist that we received from the Apostle John has always been *very, very* interesting to me, to say the least. I mean, is it not just so fascinating that somehow, someway this Lofty Lunatic of Lucifer will someday suffer a deadly wound – actually experience *death* – and then rise back into life completely restored and healed as if nothing ever happened? Wow, my eyes open wide in amazement every time I think of this upcoming, astonishing, and factual event that will undoubtedly and understandably shock everyone who will one day witness this diabolical and indescribable occurrence. So, at this time, let's go ahead and take a look at the three scriptures in God's word that speak of this incredible, unforgettable, and eye-opening event:

"And I saw one of his heads as it were

Wounded to death; and his deadly
Wound was healed..."
Revelation 13: 3

"...whose [the antichrist's] deadly
Wound was healed."
Revelation 13: 12

"which [the antichrist] had the
Wound by a sword, and did live."
Revelation 13: 14

First, I'd like to say that apparently I'm not the only one who believes that three supporting scriptures are enough. On a more serious note, if you have found the true meaning of the antichrist's "deadly wound" to be elusive, well, I have good news: You can now start praising the Lord with me, because God *did* show me the true meaning, and as sure as Jesus rose on the third day and is also the Savior of the world, you can take *everything* you have ever heard pertaining to this very intriguing clue and throw it all in the garbage can; that's right, you certainly can, and the sooner you do it the better.

Alright, where do I begin? I know. How about here: The theory that seems to be held by most people is that the antichrist will somehow suffer a gunshot wound to his head; that, however, is incorrect; yep, it sure is. Actually, his deadly wound is something that's a little bit different than that of a gunshot; it definitely is, and even a whole lot different would be a better way to describe it. So, having said that, are you now ready to find out the exact meaning of what the antichrist's deadly wound *really is?* Alright, well, I suggest that you sit straight up in your chair and brace yourself, because here is what will one day *really* happen; here, now, is the *actual* meaning of such an intriguing and mystifying clue that for the last 2000 years has had masses of people not just in awe like myself, but virtually in utter confusion in trying to clearly understand and correctly solve the meaning of the antichrist's deadly wound: The antichrist's "deadly wound" is a stroke, a *medical* stroke. Yes, that's right. The antichrist will one day suffer a fatal, medical stroke, an actual *disease* that will strike his brain (because that's where a medical stroke takes place) and kill him on the spot. Now, that's just amazing!

What's also very interesting and even rather helpful is the actual Greek definition for a word found in verse three (the first verse I quoted) -- the word, "healed." Boy, let me tell you, this word's meaning is absolutely *loaded* with revelation, and it also totally confirms *and* undeniably cements the irrefutable fact that the antichrist will someday suffer a fatal, medical stroke. So, are you ready to find out what it means? Ok, it literally means "...to relieve (of disease)..."[11] Yes, that's right, a *disease* is what the antichrist's deadly wound is and what he will someday suffer; it will be the disease of a stroke that will one day kill the antichrist; and how do we know that the "deadly wound" that he will suffer will be a stroke? Well, that's also in God's word , and the answer comes from the word "wound," which is found in all three of the verses that you read earlier; it's literal Greek meaning is – you guessed it -- "...a stroke..."[12] To be sure, if you're wondering whether or not a stroke is a disease, then I'm positive you'll discover that the precise answer puts an abrupt and emphatic end to any and all speculation, suggestion, or even debate suggesting that the "deadly wound" the antichrist will one day suffer is anything but a medical stroke; yep, it sure does. The answer, ladies and gentlemen, is that it is, in fact, a

---

[11] Taken from *THE NEW STRONG'S EXHAUSTIVE CONCORDANCE OF THE BIBLE* by Strong, James, LL.D., . S.T.D., 41

[12] Ibid., 72

disease. So, based on all that amazing evidence, what we have learned and can confidently say without a shadow of any doubt whatsoever is:

1. The antichrist's "deadly wound" is none other than a medical stroke.
2. The antichrist will one day be killed through a stroke.
3. The antichrist will one day be healed from the *disease* of a stroke.

Now, I must say, if finally discovering the true meaning of what the antichrist's deadly wound is after 2000 years doesn't cause you to get a little excited, then I'm very surprised. Just writing about it excites and amazes me, and God revealed it to me way back in 2008! Amazing to me also is the fact that the answer has been in God's word all along, all this time. Well, one thing's for sure: I never could nor ever would have known it if He wouldn't have so graciously and undeservedly revealed it to me; and for that I'm extremely grateful.

So far, we have correctly learned the exact meaning of the antichrist's deadly wound. Now, let's look at what God's word says that it is not:

1. It is *not* a wound resulting from a gunshot.
2. It is *not* a wound resulting from a physical, forceful blow of any kind.
3. It is *not* the disease of a bullet or the disease of any type of physical, forceful blow (Yes, sarcasm could be detected there.).

Ok, so, it should be pointed out that the word, "stroke" is used in various ways in The Holy Bible, and both the severity and the meanings differ dramatically. For example, there is a stroke of a literal sword (Esther 9:5), there's one that's literal translation is "contusion (Isaiah 30: 26),"[13] one that means in the original Hebrew language, "a blow (Psalms 39: 10),"[14] and even one that is actually not given a Hebrew definition, but is used along when a tree is cut down with an axe (Deuteronomy 19: 5). Interestingly enough, however, there *is* a "stroke" used in the very sad story involving the death of the Prophet Ezekiel's wife, and it seems to be quite similar to the eventual "wound"

---

[13] Taken from *THE NEW STRONG'S EXHAUSTIVE CONCORDANCE OF THE BIBLE* by Strong, James, LL.D., . S.T.D., 76

[14] Ibid, 90

or stroke of the antichrist. Yes, it sure does. Let's go ahead and take a look at it now:

> "Also the word of the Lord came unto me
> Saying, Son of man, behold, I take away
> From thee the desire of thine eyes with a
> Stroke. Yet neither shalt thou mourn nor
> Weep, neither shall they tears run down.
> Forbear to cry, make no mourning for the
> Dead, bind the tire of thine head upon thee,
> And put on thy shoes upon thy feet, and cover
> Not thy lips, and eat not the bread of men.
> So I spake unto the people in the morning:
> And at evening my wife died; and I did in
> The morning as I was commanded."
> Ezekiel 24: 15-18

Interesting, isn't it? Now, although there's very little information regarding Ezekiel wife's death, I'm willing to go out on a limb (this is pure speculation on my part) and say that I'm pretty sure that the good Lord did not violently bludgeon her or use the stroke of an axe or some kind of piece of wood like a table leg, for that matter, to "…take away…" her life. No, God is not mean. He's nice. He certainly wouldn't have done that. Plus, the holy scriptures *do actually say* that God did take her life "…with a stroke…" and that, ladies and gentlemen, is very intriguing as well as very significant, because the Bible through the literal translation of the word "wound" says the very, same thing about the antichrist. Well, I'll tell you what: Ezekiel wife's death and that of the antichrist are not just similar in nature but also are very interesting, to say the least.

Alright, there's just one more point that I would like to make, and then this chapter covering the incredible topic of the antichrist's deadly wound will be completely finished. The last point revolves around the word, "sword," and the word, itself, was used earlier in one of the first, supporting references; in fact, you might recall the actual verse that it was found in; it was this one right here:

> "…which [the antichrist] had the
> wound by a sword, and did live."
> Revelation 13: 14

The point that I would now like to make regarding the word, "sword," is this: The "sword" spoken of here in this verse is not -- I repeat – *not* meant as a literal sword, one, perhaps, that a person would reach out and grasp with the use of their hand or hands; no, it *absolutely* is not. Without question, the "sword" described here in this verse are the very unstoppable and invincible words of God. Here, now, is the proof:

> "And he [The Lord Jesus] had in
> His right hand seven stars: and
> Out of his mouth went a sharp
> Twoedged sword."
> Revelation 1: 16
> "Repent; or else I will come unto
> Thee quickly, and will fight against
> Them with the sword of my mouth."
> Revelation 2: 16
> "And the remnant were slain with
> The sword of him that sat upon the
> Horse, which sword proceeded out
> Of his mouth."
> Revelation 19: 21

See, the sword in verse 14 of Revelation 13 really *is* representative of the mighty and awesome words of God, and you just witnessed for yourself the absolute proof of it right there in those above, supporting references. Now, having said that, some might wonder why the Apostle John chose to call the words of God a "sword." Well,

the correct reason why is because whenever God prom-
ises harm (via His mouth, obviously), His literal words
become an unconquerable weapon of destruction – even,
in this case, an actual sword – and one, I might add, that
would easily cause anyone (if they had any real sense) to
quickly wish that they had not unwisely angered God
in the first place, as they watch in horror as He quickly
and without hesitation unsheathes and unleashes His prevailing and very dreadful sword of destructive harm from
His supreme and powerful mouth. So, that's why John
used the word "sword" to accurately describe God's words
of righteous anger, and that's also why John chose that
very sharp and potentially life-threatening instrument of
war to perfectly describe the extremely frightful and powerful words of God.

Alright, with that last point being made, this chapter is
now finished.

His Father's Name is Abraham

It certainly is. The antichrist has a father named Abraham. Ok, I now have another clue to give to you, but I must say, you might find it a little puzzling. Here it is: His physical father's name is not known at this time; no, it is not. It would be certainly nice to know the name of his physical father, the father who fathered him through conception, and not the name of his father whom he is a descendant of, for that would be, in fact, his father Abraham, but it is unknown. You see, he has two fathers; yes, two. One father is his physical father while the other father is also his father because he will be a descendant of him and, like his father, a man of Jewish descent, for he – the antichrist – will be a Jew.

Now, that saddens me. Why? Well, what I find particularly sad is the factual reality of the antichrist being of

Jewish descent and literally belonging to the *very people* that God personally and lovingly chose to be His own; that definitely is sad, but unfortunately, as fateful as it very well is, it is, indeed, the case, and it certainly can be seen within the scriptures, as you will most definitely witness and discover for yourself by continuing to turn the pages of this very book; having said that, let's go ahead and take a look at one of them right now:

> "Neither shall he regard the God
> Of his fathers..."
> Daniel 11: 37

In this verse, there is a lot to be said. First, the word "God" in its original text is used in the plural sense, meaning that *this* "God" is not made up of one, singular person, but actually consists of more than one; and this is important because the God of The Holy Bible *is* a God that consists of three holy but separate, different entities, if you will, and even a God that is summed up in *three* heavenly persons: The Holy Father, The Holy Son, and The Holy Ghost. Here's the proof:

> "For there are three that bear
> Record in Heaven, the Father,

The Word, and the Holy Ghost:
And these three are one."
1 John 5: 7

See, the God of The Holy Bible really is a God that is made up of *three,* separate persons, and each person has their own divine title and function; but allthree -- The Holy Father, The Holy Son, and The Holy Spirit – are all God.

Alright, it should be noted that when the Apostle John used the words "the Word," he was referring to none other than The Lord Jesus Christ. You can discover the very proof of this for yourself in John's book of The Holy Bible, particularly the first 18 verses.

Ok, let's continue. The word "God" in the verse "Neither shall he regard the God of his fathers..." is literally written in the original text as "Elohim," and it not only appears exclusively in God's word through the first five chapters but even at other times when "God" is written. Therefore, one should easily say and factually conclude that "Elohim" is, in fact, the very first name of God given in His word, and it is also the name of God that we are introduced to when we meet Him in His word for the very first time.

The next and last part in the verse, "Neither shall he regard the God of his fathers..." that I would now like to address is the last word -- "...fathers..." Here and many times before, without a shadow of *any* doubt, the Prophet Daniel was clearly and, in fact, very obviously making a reference to some of the patriarchs of The Nation of Israel, the forefathers Abraham, Isaac, and Jacob, to be exact. Daniel used the word "fathers," because God actually made a covenant with those three men; and as documented in His word itself, it was a very common thing for the covenant fathers (Abraham, Isaac, and Jacob) to be referenced at times. Here, you see for yourself:

> "And God said moreover unto Moses,
> Thus shalt thou say unto the children
> Of Israel, The Lord God of thy fathers,
> The God of Abraham, the God of Isaac,
> And the God of Jacob..."
> Exodus 3: 15

> "that thou mayest dwell in the land
> Which the Lord sware unto thy fathers,
> To Abraham, to Isaac, and to Jacob..."
> Deuteronomy 30: 20

Well, so far we have looked at only one verse clearly proving the antichrist to be of Jewish descent. We have our work cut out for us. Here's the next supporting reference:

> "Yet thou shalt be brought down to
> Hell, to the sides of the pit. They
> That see thee shall narrowly look
> Upon thee, and consider thee, saying,
> Is this the man that made the earth
> To tremble, that did shake kingdoms;
> That made the world as a wilderness,
> And destroyed the cities thereof; that
> Opened not the house of his Prisoners?
> All the kings of the nations, even all of
> them, lie in glory, every one in his own
> house. But that art cast out
> Of thy grave like an abominable branch,
> And as the raiment of those that are
> Slain, thrust through with a sword, that
> Go down to the stones of the pit; as
> A carcase trodden under feet. Thou
> Shalt not be joined with them in
> Burial, because thou hast destroyed
> Thy land, and slain thy people..."
> Isaiah 14: 15-20

Where I would like to comment first is on the earlier part of this supporting reference, specifically where it says, "… Is this the man…" Here the prophecy the Prophet Isaiah is speaking about is clearly directed to the antichrist, for the antichrist is, in fact, a *man;* that's right, the antichrist is a man; he's not an angel (definitely not an angel); he's not a demon; he's 100%, absolutely a *man.*

Now, some people have incorrectly stated that these verses pertain to Satan, but the problem with that notion is that Satan is *not* a "man." He's an angel and a fallen one at that; so, this verse *unquestionably* is directed to that Lofty Lunatic of Lucifer, the antichrist.

Question: Did you happen to notice what the scriptures said regarding whose land and whose people that this "man" will destroy? It said that both the land and the people were none other than *his,* of his very own race – hence, the word "thy" was used in the text. So, again, God's word steadfastly and clearly points out that the antichrist will attempt to destroy both *his* land and *his* people. Would you like the proof? Ok, here it is:

> "And his [the antichrists] power
> Shall be mighty, but not by his own

Power; and he shall destroy wonder-
Fully, and shall prosper, and prac-
Tise, and shall destroy the mighty
And the holy people [the people
Of Israel]."
Daniel 8: 24

"Behold, the day of the Lord cometh,
And thy spoil shall be divided in the
Midst of thee. For I will gather all
Nations against Jerusalem to battle;
And the city shall be taken, and the
Houses rifled, and the women
Ravished; and half of the city shall
Go forth into captivity..."
Zechariah 14: 1-2

Alright, we're moving right along. Here is the next supporting reference, irrefutably proving the antichrist to, in fact, be of Jewish descent:

"And thou, profane wicked prince
Of Israel, whose day is come, when
Iniquity shall have an end..."
Ezekiel 21: 25

Regarding this verse, I would say that the obvious, first part up for discussion would be God's word addressing the antichrist, calling him, "profane" and "wicked" and even going much further than that by actually proving to us that not only will the antichrist become the "prince of Israel" one day, but in doing so, he must also be a Jew. Why do I say that? Well, simply because the antichrist *cannot* – I repeat *cannot* – be the "prince of Israel" and *not* be Jewish; no, he can't. Rather, what God is saying here in this verse is that the antichrist *must* be a Jew, because he will one day be Israel's King. Therefore, I feel that this verse should cause one to very easily conclude that the antichrist absolutely must be -- *without question* – a Jew; oh, would you like the very proof of this? Alright, here it is:

> "When thou art come unto the land
> Which the Lord thy God giveth thee,
> And shall possess it, and shalt dwell
> Therein, and shalt say, I will set a
> King over me, like as all the nations
> That are about me; Thou shalt in
> Any wise set hi king over thee.
> Whom the Lord thy God shall choose:
> One from among thy brethren shalt

Thou set king over thee: thou
Mayest not set a stranger over
thee, which is not thy brother."
Deuteronomy 17: 14-15

See, there's the proof right there, undeniably proving without a shadow of any doubt, that the antichrist who will one day become King of Israel will *absolutely* be of Jewish descent; it – or The Lord, rather, through His word – says so right there in that verse, plainly and adamantly telling The Nation of Israel that their King *must* be "...from among thy brethren..." and that they "...mayest not set a stranger [a foreigner, someone not of Israeli descent] over thee, which is not thy brother." See, there's the proof right there. There's all the proof you'll ever really need to see as well as completely understand that the antichrist unquestionably will be of Jewish descent.

Alright, I think right now would be a good time to go ahead and submit the literal proof of the antichrist actually becoming Israel's King; so, here it is:

"And he [the antichrist] shall con-
Firm the covenant with many

[Israel] for one week."
Daniel 9: 27

Yeah, I know. I know this verse is kind of confusing, but please allow me to help by hopefully making it a little more understandable. The word, "he" speaks of that Lofty Lunatic of Lucifer, the antichrist. The covenant Daniel speaks of here is the seven year peace pact that Israel, once selecting the antichrist as their *Jewish* King, will make exclusively with him; and the last part of this verse that is going to now be addressed is where Israel is literally referenced; it is directly referenced with the word, "many" as in the antichrist will one day, evidently, make a number of peace covenants with Israel no doubt being one of his *many* partners. So, having said all that, one could – and should, for that matter – correctly read the verse as follows: "And he [the antichrist] shall confirm the [peace] covenant with many [Israel]..;" and, again, by him doing so, it absolutely proves that the antichrist will definitely be of Jewish descent. Oh, but wait! As if you still needed more evidence proving the antichrist to be of Jewish descent, here, now, are some more scriptural references literally proving the antichrist to be a king:

"And the king [the antichrist]

Shall do according to his will;"
Daniel 11: 36

"And in the latter time of their
Kingdom, when the trangressors
Are come to the full, a king [the
Antichrist] ...shall stand up."
Daniel 8: 23

"And I {the Apostle John] saw,
And behold a white horse; and he
[the antichrist] that sat on him had
A bow; and a crown was given unto
Him; and he went forth conquering
And to conquer."
Revelation 6: 2

Alright, the next part of the supporting reference (Ezekiel 21: 25; If need be, please turn back to view it.) that will now be discussed is what is meant by "whose day is come;" this means that one day in the future, the antichrist will meet God in battle and will be completely defeated in every sense of the word. Scriptural references literally and clearly proving the antichrist's upcoming day of defeat can be found in the first thirteen verses of Chapter 39 in the Book of Ezekiel.

The remaining part of the verse, "when iniquity shall have an end" actually has a double meaning which is *totally* not uncommon in God's word, as you will no doubt discover a little later. The meaning here speaks of the antichrist's wicked, ungodly acts that he will one day commit but will ultimately "...have an end." The other meaning, believe it or not, speaks of a truly wonderful time like no other that will one day happen but only for God's children – The Millenium (You can find scriptural evidence of The Millenium in Isaiah 2: 1-4 and Zephaniah 3: 9-13.) Now, as I was saying, we know with all certainty from God's word that the following offenses are just some but certainly not all of his despicable, iniquitous acts:

- He will cause destruction even for his people, the Jews (Daniel 8: 24).
- He will cause "deceit to prosper (Daniel 8: 25)."
- He will oppose God, claim that he really is God, And even sit in God's temple (2 Thessalonians 2: 4)
- He will receive worship from the people on earth (Revelation 13: 3,4)

- He will blaspheme God, God's domain, and even The people who are in Heaven (Revelation 13: 6).
- He will even attempt, as we learned earlier, to Slay the Lord Jesus Himself but will be thoroughly Destroyed (Daniel 8: 25).

Alright, as mentioned earlier, God's word absolutely carries a double meaning some times, and in an effort to further prove and even cement the fact that at times His word really does address a particular person with a name that, from just looking on the surface, doesn't appear to belong or apply, here, now, is a scriptural passage where God is speaking directly to Satan through the addressment of Eloth III, the King of Tyrus:

> "Moreover the word of the Lord
> Came unto me, saying, Son of man,
> Take up a lamentation upon the king
> Of Tyrus, and say unto him, Thus
> Saith the Lord God; Thou sealest up
> The sum, full of wisdom, and perfect
> In beauty. Thou hast been in Eden the
> Garden of God; every precious stone
> Was thy covering, the sardius, topaz,
> And the diamond, the beryl, the onyx,

And the jasper, the sapphire, the
Emerald, and the carbuncle, and
Gold: the workmanship of thy ta-
Brets and of thy pipes was pre-
Pared in thee in the day that thou
Wast created. Thou art the anointed
Cherub that covereth; and I have
Set thee so; thou wast upon the
Holy mountain of God; thou hast
Walked up and down in the midst
Of the stones of fire. Thou wast
Perfect in thy ways from the day
That thou wast created, till ini-
Quity was found in thee."
Ezekiel 28: 11-15

So, according to the above passage you just read, is not *Satan* the one who is "...full of wisdom, and perfect in beauty?" Well, it certainly isn't the King of Tyrus, right? Ok, and wasn't Satan the one who "...hast been in Eden the garden of God?" It definitely wasn't the King of Tyrus, wouldn't you say? Alright, and *surely* the King of Tyrus isn't the one who's covered with all those precious stones and has "...the workmanship of thy tabrets [tambourines] and of thy pipes..." built right into his being just like

Satan did "in the day that thou [he] wast created," I might add, right? *Surely*, it is Satan who is being spoken of here, right? *Surely*, it is Satan and not – *definitely* not – the King of Tyrus, *right?* Ok (this one should be really easy), surely – and without question – it is *Satan* who's "...the anointed cherub that covereth," is the one who "wast upon the holy mountain of God," and also the one who "...hast walked up and down in the midst of the stones of fire," right? *Surely and most definitely*, it was not the King Tyrus who, by all accounts, was the anointed and angelic cherubim that was granted the blessed privilege to do all those marvelous and truly unimaginable tasks for God, *right? Surely*, it is, once again, Satan who's the one being spoken of here and not – definitely not – the King of Tyrus, *right?* You know, I could go on, but, really, I think I've made the point perfectly clear, and it is this: Unquestionably, at times The Holy Bible appears to be speaking to just one person, but in reality it is actually speaking to more than just that person, just like in the earlier case where we witnessed for ourselves God's word was, indeed, speaking to the antichrist and of The Millenium at the very same time.

Ok, so there's just one more point that needs to be made, and then this chapter will be complete. The following verse, itself, is rather short, but it packs a punch and definitely proves like all the rest of the presented evidence that the antichrist will, in fact, be of Jewish descent; here, take a look:

> "and the people of the prince that
> Shall come shall destroy the city
> And the sanctuary;"
> Daniel 9: 26

See, that verse makes it very clear as to what it is actually saying. Believe it or not, in once sentence it totally proves that the antichrist will not only be Israel's "prince" but that, consequently, he will also be of Jewish descent. Notice, also, if you will, it states as well that the "prince... shall come..;" that's clearly a direct reference to the antichrist, because we all know one day he will, in fact, come.

Alright, well, with that last truth being made and, more importantly, proved, this chapter is now finished. I certainly hope that you are fully convinced like I am that the antichrist will be of Jewish descent; there really is no other legitimate conclusion to come to once all the incredible and truthful evidence is thoroughly examined and given its due diligence. Plus, I wholeheartedly believe that there is definitely *more* than enough scriptural evidence to totally prove that the antichrist really will be a Jew; but, at this point, I have to ask: Is someone in particular beginning to appeal to you, someone that comes to your mind as to who this Lofty Lunatic of Lucifer could possibly be? Perhaps it would help if you were to first review the three clues that have been presented; having said that, here they now are:

1. The antichrist will be extremely prideful.
2. The antichrist's "deadly wound" will actually be a stroke.
3. The antichrist will be of Jewish descent.

His Tribe was not Numbered

Back in the days before the Lamb of God, Jesus Christ, left His heavenly thrown traded in His supernatural body for a fleshly human one, and ultimately paid the price for our sins by being brutally sacrificed on a wooden cross, a census numbering the twelve tribes of the Nation of Israel was taken. This census, as God instructed Moses, included all of the tribes except one. This one tribe that was not numbered is where you will now find your next clue; it is the tribe of the Levites, the tribe that God Himself chose to serve him as priests, and it is the tribe of the antichrist. You see, the antichrist will one day be a priest, a priest of God, and as well, a High Priest at that. Here, now, is your first passage of scripture confirming the validity of your fourth of five clues:

> "And thou profane wicked prince of
> Israel, whose day is come when ini-
> Quity shall have an end, Thus saith
> The Lord God; Remove the diadem,
> And take off the crown; this shall not
> Be the same; exalt him who is low
> And abase him who is high."
> Ezekiel 21: 25-26

Now, I know you're probably thinking that the first verse seems a little familiar, and it should. I previously used it in the last clue, proving the antichrist to be of Jewish descent; but trust me, I'll need it later, and it happens to be irreplaceable and of tremendous value. Having said that, I feel that this verse is pretty straightforward as to what God is saying, but it's in the word "diadem" that we find proof of the antichrist one day really becoming a priest. You see, the word "diadem" makes reference to the official hat or mitre of the high priest, the same mitre that God instructed His High Priests to wear; yep, I kid you not; He sure did, and here, now, is the proof:

> "And take thou unto me Aaron thy
> Brother, and his sons with him,
> From among the children of Israel,

That he may minister unto me in the
Priests's office, even Aaron, Nadab,
And Abihu, Eleazar and Ithamar,
Aaron's sons. And thou shalt make
Holy garments for Aaron thy brother
For glory and for beauty. And thou
Shalt speak unto all that are wise
Hearted, whom I have filled with the
Spirit of wisdom, that they may make
Aaron's garments to consecrate him,
"that he may minister unto me in the
Priest's office. And these are the gar-
Ments which they shall make: a
Breastplate, and an ephod, and a
Robe, and a broidered coat, a mitre..."
Exodus 21: 1-4

See, the Lord's requirement for His priests were to wear a priestly diadem or mitre, and this was required *only* – let me repeat that – *only* for his priests. As for God telling the antichrist to "take of the crown," we already know that the antichrist will not only be a king but a Jewish one at that; and as the two iron-clad, prophetic facts were earlier fully established in the previous chapter, they are, once again, proven and even thoroughly cemented here in this verse.

What is meant by "this shall not be the same" is that God very clearly and totally disapproves with the antichrist taking on both offices of Israel's Priesthood and Kingship, as you will no doubt see for yourself a little later.

Now, some people have erroneously thought that this particular verse addresses King Zedekiah, the Southern King of Israel at the time of the Babylonian invasion; however, this cannot be true, and the reason why is because the verse clearly states that both the crown of the king *and* the diadem or mitre of the priest are being worn; and with all due respect, King Zedekiah, in his personal history of being Israel's King, *never* took on both offices, the office of the priesthood and of the king at the same time, nor did he ever even attempt to do such a feat. Therefore, the "profane" and "wicked' king here in this verse is not nor can it possibly be Zedekiah; it *is*, however, the antichrist, who, according to Dr. Willmington, will, indeed, one day take on both of those two distinct offices:

> "The antichrist will attempt (unsuc-
> cesfully) to combine the three Old
> Testament offices of prophet, priest,

And king, as someday Christ will
Successfully do."[15]

Next up, this part of the verse: "exalt him that is low and abase him thatis High." Ok, I'll give you one guess – just one – as to who the word "him" in this verse is directed towards (Hint: This person is the complete opposite of Moses.). On a more serious note, this part of the verse is just another piece of evidence and overwhelming testament to the first clue that was presented to you; you know, the one about the antichrist being so lofty, arrogant, and full of pride; yeah, that one. Well, here's just another of God's scriptures, once again, wholeheartedly proving the antichrist to be beyond conceited, and, in the process, cementing even further the validity, truthfulness, and soundness of that first clue. As for the meaning of the verse, God is saying that He wants to and, in fact, will "abase" the antichrist, meaning He will not only just destroy the antichrist but will actually thoroughly humiliate him. No doubt God is earnestly looking forward to the day when Him and the antichrist will meet face to face in battle; here's the proof:

---

[15] Dr. H.L. Willmington, *"Willmington's Guide to the Bible"* (Wheaton: Tyndale House Publishers, Inc., 1984), 566

"The Lord shall laugh at him; for
He seeth that his day is coming."
Psalm 37: 13

Earlier, I said that at a later time we would further discuss God's disapproval concerning the antichrist taking on both the office of the king and of the priest; well, now's that time. Please allow me to first say, however, that the verse you will read next is a continuation of the last supporting reference, but I felt it would be easier on the both of us to just go ahead and quote it once again. I hope this helps:

"And thou profane wicked prince
Of Israel, whose day is come when
Iniquity shall have an end, Thus
Saith the Lord God; Remove the
Diadem, and take off the crown;
This shall not be the same; exalt
Him who is low, and abase him
Who is high. I will overturn,
Overturn, overturn, it: and it shall
Be no more, until he come whose
Right it is; and I will give it to him."
Ezekiel 21: 25-27

You can certainly see God's course of action as well as how much He really disapproves of the antichrist taking on both offices, the office of the king and of the priest. Clearly, His absolute disapproval is seen in the word "overturn" and the fact that it was emphatically used *three* times. Now, check this out; you'll love this: There's a hidden meaning in this part of the verse; yes, that's right, a significant, hidden meaning. Did you happen to see it? Did you? Well, believe me, it's there; and here it is: As Jewish history would have it, there were other additional Kings of Israel who found out the hard way just how much God disapproves and is displeased with someone taking on both offices, the office of the priesthood and the king. Now, care to guess how many kings? Well, in fact, there were *three* kings; that's right, three. And how many times did God say he would "overturn" someone trying to take on both offices? Three! Wow! That is so cool and meaningful! God is Amazing!

So, like I said, three kings in Jewish history sought out the office of both the priesthood and of the king and – get this – *all three* received severe punishment for doing so; they were none other than King Jeroboam, King Saul, and King Uzziah. Dr. Willmington fantastically elaborates:

"Jeroboam visits the altar in Bethel To burn incense. He now becomes The second of three Israelite Kings Who dared to take upon themselves The office of the priest also. All three Were severely punished. The other Two were:

a. Saul (1 Samuel 13: 9-14)
b. Uzziah (2 Chronicles 26: 16-21)

For his idolatry, Jeroboam is prophesied against and punished by a man of God.

a. The prophecy. That years later
A king of Judah named Josiah
Would totally destroy Jeroboam's
False religion, even burning the
Bones of his dead priests upon the
Very altar where Jeroboam stood
Sacrificing. This amazing prophecy
Was fulfilled exactly some 300 years
Later. (Compare 1 Kings 13: 2 with
2 Kings 23: 15, 16.)

b. The punishment. Jeroboam's altar
Was destroyed and his arm was
Paralyzed, both supernaturally

From God (1 Kings 13: 3-6)…God
Strikes Jeroboam with a plague
And he dies after a wicked reign
Of twenty-two years. No less than
No less than twenty-two times it is
Recorded that he "made Israel to
Sin."[16]

Obviously, God was referencing these three kings when He spoke the word "overturn" exactly *three* times, and He was also sending a message, a threat even, to the antichrist not to do the same.

Ok, the next part of the supporting reference that we will now take a look at is this one right here:

> "and it shall be no more, until he
> Come whose right it is; and I will
> Give it to him."

"and it shall be no more" -- I think the meaning here is pretty obvious. God is saying that after the antichrist is thoroughly dealt with or "abased (verse 25)," never again

---

[16] Ibid., 150-151

will the antichrist or someone else, for that matter, hold the offices of both the priesthood and the king except "until he come whose right it is; and I will give it to him." The "he" here in that verse is none other than the Lord Jesus, and God is saying two things: His Son, Jesus, will one day hold both positions of the priesthood and of the kingship (one), and, that it is, indeed, *His* "right" to both of those respective offices (two); and since it is His right, God will, therefore, "give it to him."

Scriptural evidence of the Lord Jesus forthcoming priesthood and kingship can be found in the following passages: Hebrews 7: 14-28; Luke 1: 26-33.

Ok, we're moving right along. Let's continue, but please first allow me to preface the upcoming passage. The "Assyrian" and, as mentioned earlier, "the bough," are direct references to the antichrist. Here, now, is your next supporting reference, proving, once again, beyond a shadow of any doubt the antichrist to unquestionably be a high priest one day:

> "Therefore thus saith the Lord God
> Of hosts, O my people that dwellest
> In Zion, be not afraid of the Assyrian;

He shall smite thee with a rod, and
Shall lift up his staff against thee, af-
Ter the manner of Egypt. For yet a
Very little while, and the indignation
Shall cease, and mine anger in their
Destruction. And the Lord of hosts
Shall stir up a scourge for him according
To the slaughter of Midian at the rock
Of Oreb; and as his rod was upon the
Sea, so shall he lift it up after the man-
Ner of Egypt. And it shall come to pass
In that day that his burden shall be ta-
Ken away from off thy shoulder, and
his yoke from off thy neck, and the yoke
Shall be destroyed because of the
Anointing. He is come to Aiath, he is
Passed to Migron, at Michmash he
Hath laid up his carriages: They are
Gone over the passage; they have
Taken up their lodging at Geba; Ra-
Mah is afraid; Gibeah of saul is fled.
Lift up thy voice, O daughter of Gal-
Lim: cause it to be heard unto Laish,
O poor Anathoth. Madmenah is re-
Moved; the inhabitants of Gebim ga-

Ther themselves to flee. As yet shall
He remain at Nob that day; he shall
Shake his hand against the mount of
The daughter of Zion, the hill of Jerusalem.
Behold, the Lord, the Lord of hosts, shall
Lop the bough with terror: and the high
Ones of stature shall be hewn down,
And the haughty shall be humbled."
Isaiah 10: 24-33

As proven earlier, God's word sometimes has a double meaning, and while it is addressing one person, it can also at the *same time* be addressing someone else. Well, the above passage in Isaiah 10 is no different; it, too, has a double meaning, and it, at the very same time while speaking directly to the Assyrian king, King Sennacharib (Isaiah 36: 1), also speaks directly to that Lofty Lunatic of Lucifer, the antichrist; yep, it certainly does, and here's where it gets *very* interesting, to say the least: This passage, says God, is the actual route that the antichrist will one day in the future take, and you can now thank the good Lord with me, because Pastor Jimmy Swaggart will now personally attest to this very true prophetic occurrence:

"in a Passage of magnificent poetic Prophesy

In verses 28 to 32, Isaiah, in a vision, describes
The approach of the Antichrist and his host
Against Jerusalem."[17]

Now, there are no less than eighteen towns or places mentioned; some are even repeated. Personally, it would not be
surprising to me at all if someone were to become bored
or even lost (That would be me. Without Him revealing
this passage's true and exact meaning, I definitely would
have been lost for sure.) while reading that passage, given
all those towns and places. Anyway, having said that, what
I would like to do now is ask you a few questions, questions that pertain to one specific town in particular. So,
do you remember the name of the town that will end the
antichrist's route, the town he will not only stop at but
actually "remain" in? Now, why do you think that out of all
those towns in the land of Israel, the antichrist will stop
and "remain" there? I'll tell you why (Personally, I find
the answer to be not just astonishing but also incredible;
it truly is a juicy tidbit.): The name of that town that the
antichrist will one day stop at and remain in is Nob; and
why the City of Nob is *so* extremely important, and what

---

[17] Jimmy Swaggart, *"The Expositor's Study Bible"* (Baton Rouge: Jimmy
Swaggart Ministries, 2010), 1120

is *so absolutely incredible* about the City of Nob is that *this* city – out of all the cities in Israel – was *exclusively* for one, specific tribe of the Jews; *this* city was for the tribe of the Levites; *this* city was for the Levitical Priests. Wow! Now, that's just absolutely amazing! Here, now, is the proof:

> "And Nob, the city of the priests..."
> 1 Samuel 22: 19

See, God is prophetically saying that the antichrist will one day dwell in the city of Nob and "remain" there; and why will he remain there? Oh, that's simple: Because he's a Levite, a priest; *that's* why; *that's* why he will one day remain in Nob. See, I told you that the answer would be incredible, amazing, and nothing short of astonishing! See, I told you!

Alright, we're almost done with the fourth of five clues. Here, now, is the last supporting reference, proving the antichrist to, in fact, be a Levitical Priest (Please allow me to quickly preface this passage by saying that "...the beast..." is just another name for the antichrist, and "...he..." is the antichrist's helper; yes, that's right, the anti-christ will really have someone helping him. The evidence of this can discovered in Revelation 13: 11-15.):

"And he causeth all, both small and
 Great, rich and poor, free and bond,
 To receive a mark in their right
 Hand, or in their foreheads: and
 That no man might buy or sell, save
 He that had the mark, or the name
 Of the beast, or the number of his
 Name."
Revelation 13: 16-17

According to this verse, if you are stuck here on earth with the antichrist and his evil buddy, and you refuse to get your forehead or your right hand marked with his name or the number of his name, you and your actions will be *extremely* limited. Literally, God's word tells us that you will not be able to "...buy or sell." Now, that definitely is extreme. I mean, imagine not being able to buy gas for your car or bread for your meal and also not being able to sell or, for that matter, pawn your old, dusty, gold chain that had been kept in your sock drawer for the past three years. Imagine that! Wow, one would certainly be in need of a bit of good luck; that's for sure. All kidding aside, what I find particularly interesting about this passage is the location of the antichrist's mark: the forehead or the right hand. I find the location interesting, because

God required His Jewish Priests to both administer and receive markings of blood and even of oil on the thumb of their right hand (the same hand that the antichrist will require) and to also have His name (albeit on a ascribed plate of gold) on their forehead – also just like the antichrist (his name, that is) will evidently one day require. Here's the proof:

"And the priest shall take some of
The blood of the trespass offering,
And the priest shall put it upon...the
Thumb of his right hand..."
Leviticus 14: 14

"Then shalt thou kill the ram, and
Take of his blood, and put it upon...the
Thumb of their right hand."
Exodus 29: 20

"And thou shalt make a plate of pure
Gold, and grave upon it, like the
Engravings of a signet, HOLINESS
TO THE LORD. And thou shalt put
It on a blue lace, that it may be
Upon the mitre; upon the forefront

> Of the mitre it shall be. And it shall
> Be upon Aaron's forehead, that
> Aaron may bear the iniquity of the
> Holy things, which the children of
> Israel shall hallow in all their holy
> Gifts; and it shall be always upon his
> Forehead, that they may be accepted
> Before the Lord."
> Exodus 28: 36-38

You know, I've heard many pastors tell me that what God does, Satan will always try to copy. Well, from the above passage, we clearly see a perfect example of that. The antichrist, being a Levitical Priest himself, will, evidently, require pretty much the same exact thing of his followers that God had requested of His Levitical Priests.

Well, having said that, clue number four is now complete.

The Wages of
Sin are Death

Earlier, we learned that God has several names and that the very first name of God, as it appears in His word, is Elohim. Well, I can easily say that Elohim is a good God; He really is. His love for you and I is truly amazing; and it is also very deep and so much that if we were to try to measure it, it would extend far past the moon and into the Milky Way, all the way up to Heaven itself where love radiates and beams out from His glorious being, as He humbly sits on His beautiful throne, gently and tenderly calling your name with His outstretched, loving arms, all the while being surrounded by an amazing, emerald rainbow and majestically arrayed in a magnificent, holy, and indescribable light that's gloriously filled with a encompassing peace that passes all understanding and an matchless presence so perfect and so complete that it gladly fills every void, every emptiness and, yes, heals every painful hurt or deep, emotional scar a human being could ever possibly have with the total fulfillment of meaning, purpose, and completeness of life that cannot be found anywhere else except in the one person, Elohim.

That is exactly what God wants and wishes our relationship with Him to be like at all times, but the unfortunate reality is that as long as we foolishly choose to do wrong by disobeying Him, we cause sin to get between Him and us; and while He still loves us and always will love us, the payment required with sin now in the picture is sometimes one of pain, guilt, isolation, humiliation, regret, loss, and sometimes even death.

Unfortunately for the Levites, the tribe chosen by God Himself to personally serve Him as His priests, something far greater, far worse than death itself will be the ultimate result of their selfish and unwise choice to sin, something, in fact, so horrible, so unimaginable that had it not been for the scriptures, *no one* – that's right – *no one* would ever have even dreamed of it. What is it? "It," ladies and gentlemen, is a curse, a curse representing the wages of sin belonging to the Levitical Priests, an actual God-ordained curse that will one day be placed on one, specific Levitical Priest in particular, and a curse known exclusively to all mankind for the last 2000 years as the antichrist. Here, now, is the proof:

> "The earth mourneth and fadeth away,
> The world languisheth and fadeth a-
> Way, the haughty people of the earth
> Do languish. The earth also is defiled
> Under the inhabitants thereof; be-
> Cause they have transgressed the laws,
> Changed the ordinace, broken the
> Everlasting covenant. Therefore hath
> The curse [the antichrist] devoured
> The earth, and they that dwell therein
> Are desolate..."
> Isaiah 24: 4-6

> "For my sword shall be bathed in heaven:
> Behold, it shall come down upon Idumea,
> And upon the people of my curse [the
> Antichrist], to judgment."
> Isaiah 34: 5

> "Thy first father hath sinned, and thy
> Teachers have transgressed against me.

Therefore I have profaned the princes
of the sanctuary, and have given Jacob
To the curse [the antichrist], and Israel
To reproaches."
Isaiah 43: 27-28

Now, if God speaking curses is somewhat difficult for you to grasp, it really ought not to be; no, it shouldn't. Remember, if sin is willfully embraced in our lives, and we refuse to humble ourselves and repent, then we are leaving ourselves open to being disciplined by our Heavenly Father and, thus, experiencing all sorts of unwanted trouble, from some sort of a pesky nuisance all the way to even experiencing an actual God-given curse. God says so Himself:

"As many as I love, I rebuke and
Chasten: be zealous therefore,
And repent."
Revelation 3: 19

The righteous Lord through the Apostle Paul also says:

"But we are sure that the judgment of
God is according to truth against them

Which commit such things. And thinkest
Thou this, O man, that judgest them which
Do such things, and doest the same, that
Thou shalt escape the judgment of God?
Or despises thou the riches of his good-
Ness and forbearance and longsuffering;
Not knowing that the goodness of God
Leadeth thee to repentance? But after
Thy hardness and impenitent heart
Treasurest up unto thyself wrath against
The day of wrath and revelation of the
Righteous judgment of God; Who will
Render to every man according to his
Deeds: To them who by patient contin-
uance in well doing seek for glory and
Honour and immortality, eternal life:
But unto them that are contentious,
And do not obey the truth, but obey
Unrighteousness, indignation and wrath,
Tribulation and anguish, upon every
Soul of man that doeth evil, of the Jew
First, and also of the Gentile."
Romans 2: 2-9

Alright, in the following passage, the Lord Jesus actually speaks a curse, albeit on a fig tree, but, nonetheless, He did, and He obviously felt that a curse was necessary to be spoken even from His *very own mouth:*

> "Now in the morning as he [the Lord
> Jesus] returned into the city, he
> Hungered. And when he saw a fig
> Tree in the way, he came to it, and
> Found nothing thereon, but leaves
> Only, and said unto it, Let no fruit
> Grow on thee henceforward for ever,
> And presently the fig tree withered
> Away."
> Matthew 21: 18-19

Incidentally, I feel that it should be noted that it is a well-known fact that the fig tree here in this passage is a picture of the Nation of Israel. So, with that being said, Jesus was not just casting a curse on some barren tree. He was actually cursing the Nation of Israel itself.

Now, the following two supporting references really make it very easy to accept that sin absolutely, without question can even bring death into the life of an unrepentant individual; here, you take a look for yourself:

> "The soul that sinneth, it shall die."
> Ezekiel 18: 20

> "If any man see his brother sin a sin
> Which is not unto death, he shall ask,
> And he shall give them life for them
> That sin not unto death. There is a sin
> Unto death: I do not say that he shall
> pray for it."
> 1 John 5: 16

Alright, believe it or not, God through His prophet Malachi actually spoke of cursing the Levitical Priests – He sure did -- and you can see the very proof of this truth right here:

> "And now, O ye priests, this command-
> Ment is for you. If ye will not hear, and
> If ye will not lay it to heart, to give glory
> Unto my name, saith the Lord of hosts,
> I will even send a curse [the antichrist]
> Upon you, and I will curse your blessings;

71

> Yea, I have cursed them already, because
> Ye do not lay it to heart. Behold, I will
> Corrupt your seed, and spread dung
> Upon your faces, even the dung of
> Your solemn feasts; and one shall
> Take you away with it."
> Malachi 2: 1-3

I must say, what I find particularly interesting about the above passage is how God actually says that He will curse the priests by corrupting "their seed," their offspring, and that one of their very own seed will actually, in fact, take them "away with it." Whoa! Now, that's significant right there! It sure is! Hhhmm, I wonder if that "one" God is speaking of here could really be the forthcoming antichrist. I think so. Yes, I sure do.

Alright, would you believe that even Moses knew and personally warned the Levitical Priests not only about their overall willingness to transgress against God and His word, but he also warned them about their rebellious nature and their *future* transgressions that they will one day commit? He sure did, and you can see it right here:

"And it came to pass, when Moses had

Made an end of writing the words of this
Law in a book, until they were finished,
That Moses commanded the Levites,
Which bare the ark of the covenant of
The Lord, saying, Take this book of the
Law, and put it in the side of the ark of
The covenant of the Lord your God, that
It may be there for a witness against thee.
For I know thy rebellion, and thy stiff neck:
Behold, while I am yet alive with you this
Day, ye have been rebellious against the
Lord; and how much more after my death?
Gather unto me all the elders of your
Tribes, and your officers, that I may speak
These words in their ears, and call heaven
And earth to record against them. For
I know that after my death ye will ut-
Terly corrupt [yourselves], and turn a-
Side from the way which I have com-
Maded you; and evil will befall you in
The latter days; because ye will do evil
In the sight of the Lord, to provoke
Him to anger through the work of your
Hands."
Deuteronomy 31: 24-29

Whoa! See, I told you! I told you that Moses warned the Levitical Priests; but did you see what Moses said would happen as a result of their sin? Did you? He said that evil will befall them "...in the latter days;" Now, that statement is, obviously, *very* meaningful as well as entirely significant; yep, it sure is! In effect, Moses is saying that due to the sin of the priests, evil will come upon them in the end times; obviously, the evil that Moses was speaking of is a direct reference to the antichrist; that's what he was saying; that's what Moses meant, and, surely, everyone knows that the antichrist will *certainly* be evil; he also, by the way, will be astonishingly revealed in the end times, latter days. Well, one thing's for sure: Those riveting statements made by Moses concerning the Levitical Priests' sin are definitely *very, very* incriminating, to say the least.

Well, guess what? In the following, holy passage, God, once again, speaks of the Levite's sin that they committed against Him, and here it is:

> "Thus saith the Lord God...the
> Levites that are gone away far from
> Me, when Israel went astray, which
> Went astray away from me after their
> Idols; they shall even bear their ini-

Quity. because they ministered unto
Them [people] before their [the
Levite's] idols, and caused the house
Of Israel to fall into iniquity; therefore
Have I lifted up mine hand against
Them, saith the Lord God, and they
Shall bear their iniquity. And they
Shall not come near unto me, to
Do the office of the priest unto me,
Nor to come near to any of my holy
Things, in the most holy place; but
They shall bear their shame, and
Their abominations which they
Have committed."
Ezekiel 44: 9-10; 12-13

Alright, at this point, I feel that some things should be stated and they are as follows: Although God really has placed a curse in the form of human flesh (the antichrist) specifically on the Tribe of Levi, the unfortunate reality is that the curse also reaches out and affects the entire Nation of Israel; this, along with many other reasons, is because – in His eyes—the entire nation, both priests and, as a whole, everyone else, is guilty of sinning against their God.

Also, just because God chose to speak a curse on the Levitical Priests, it does in *no* way diminish, scar, or negatively affect His wonderful, perfect, beautiful, correct, undeserved, holy and just, pure love for His chosen people; nope, it sure doesn't. The point is this: God loves His people, and He still has an outstanding (in both senses of the word) plan for them; however, this plan does, unfortunately, include the Curse of the Levitical Priests – the antichrist – and a plan that He will no doubt personally see to the very end.

Lastly, although God retains the right to discipline His children, in no way does it reflect His wonderful, holy, and perfect character in a bad way. No, it surely doesn't. God *is* perfect *and* pure *and* holy *and* just, and if one were to feel that His ways or actions aren't the exact way how they would do them, then they should just remember that *He's* the One who is God, they're not, and these choice words from the Lord Himself:

> "For my thoughts are not your thoughts,
> neither are your ways my ways, saith
> The Lord. For as the heavens are higher
> Than the earth, so are my ways higher
> Than your ways, and my thoughts than

Your thoughts."
Isaiah 55: 8-9

Ok, let's go ahead and now take a look at what the Prophet Zechariah has to say about the antichrist; and, boy, let me tell you, he certainly has a lot; but we won't be looking at everything, just one segment. In his book, he is shown several visions, and is even given an angel to explain the true meaning of what Zechariah is seeing. Well, in chapter five, Zechariah witnesses the very thing you are right now reading about; that's right; he sees the Curse of the Levitical Priests; and now you, too, will also be given the rare opportunity to get up close and personal with that cursed, despicable beast; here it is (Please note that "he" in the following passage is Zechariah's helper, the angel.):

> "Then I turned, and lifted up mine eyes,
> And looked, and behold a flying roll.
> And he said unto me, What seest thou?
> And I answered, I see a flying roll; the
> Length thereof is twenty cubits, and
> The breadth thereof ten cubits. Then
> Said he unto me, This is the curse that
> Goeth forth over the face of the whole

Earth; for every one that stealeth shall
Be cut off as on this side according to
It; and everyone that sweareth shall
Be cut off as on that side according to
It. I will bring it forth, saith the Lord of
Of hosts, and it shall enter into the house
Of the thief, and into the house of him
That sweareth falsely by my name: and
It shall remain in the midst of his house,
And shall consume it with the timber
Thereof and the stones thereof."
Zechariah 5: 1-4

The first thing that I would like to point out is that the angel refers to the flying roll as, "the curse." Gee, I wonder *who* he's referring to there. Secondly, the curse's freedom: It is able to fly "over the face of the whole earth," meaning it is not subject to just one location; it is literally flying over the entire world and, therefore, can reach all parts and all people of every nation just like the antichrist will one day be able to as well (You will no doubt read more of this later.) Ok, let's move on. "I will bring it forth," says God, meaning that it is, in fact, Him who will produce, as the angel so helpfully pointed out, "the curse."

Besides the previous scriptures that I quoted, the Apostle Paul in his letter to the church in Thessalonica gives another perspective as to why the antichrist will appear and, at the same time, proves even the more that it really will be God Who will one day "bring it [The Curse of the Levitical Priests, the antichrist] forth." Here, you see for yourself (Please note that "they" are the people who will be alive when the antichrist comes forth.):

> "...because they received not the love
> Of the truth, that they might be saved.
> And for this cause God shall send them
> Strong delusion, that they should believe
> A lie: That they all might be damned who
> Believed not the truth, but had pleasure
> In unrighteousness."
> 2 Thessalonians 2: 10-12

Most definitely, I should note that "the truth" in that awesome passage you just read is absolutely a direct reference to the Savior, the Lord Jesus. While wrapped in human flesh, He told some people (and still does through various methods) exactly who is "the truth" and where He can be found:

"Jesus saith unto him, I am the way,
The truth, and the life: no man
Cometh unto the Father, but by
Me."
John 14: 6

So, yes, as it was previously pointed out, God, the Father is the One who will "bring it [The Curse of the Levitical Priests] forth" as a result of the willful, unrepentant sin of the priests and of the people who reject "the truth," the Lord Jesus.

Next in that Zechariah passage, we are told that the curse will "enter into the house of the thief." Without question, "the thief" is none other than the devil. Here, now, is the proof:

"The thief [Satan] cometh not, but for to
Steal, and to kill, and to destroy:"
John 10: 10

We continue: The curse will, according to Zechariah's helper (the angel), "enter into the house of the thief," meaning that the devil will wholeheartedly welcome and fully accept the curse and likewise also for the curse, the antichrist – hence, the curse will "enter into" his (Satan's) house. Plus, The Holy Bible plainly and very clearly tells us in no uncertain terms where the curse can be found:

> "The curse of the Lord is in the house
> Of the wicked..."
> Proverbs 3: 3

Also, the Apostle Paul through the Holy Spirit clearly states that the thief, Satan, energizes and is in one accord with the curse, the antichrist (Please note that "him" is the antichrist.):

> "Even him, whose coming is after the
> Working of Satan with all power and
> Signs and lying wonders..."
> 2 Thessalonians 2: 9

The angel then tells Zechariah that the curse enters "into the house of him that sweareth falsely by my name." This statement is basically one very large clue. Translation: The curse enters into a Levite's house, meaning it is a *Levitical Priest* that will gladly accept this curse, The Curse of the Levitical Priests. Question: How does the verse mean that a priest will one day take on this curse? Well, the verse means it by saying, "him that sweareth falsely by my name." You see, the Lord's Priests are the ones who primarily would say or "sweareth" in God's name, as you probably have even already noticed yourself in some of the previous scripture quotations; they – the priests – would say, "Thus saith the Lord..." So, that's how we know for an absolute fact that the "him that sweareth falsely by my name" unquestionably means that it is a Levitical Priest who will one day take on the Curse of the Levitical Priests. Lastly, we are told by the angel that the curse remains "in the midst of his house, and shall consume it with the timber thereof and the stones thereof; this means that the Levitical Priest will not only take on this curse and fully accept it, but he will actually become it, build it, and develop it; another words, in every way possible, he will *totally* devote himself to this curse with absolutely no hesitation, no remorse, or no regret at all. He will, for all intents and purposes, do what the Loving Savior of the World, Jesus Christ, did not; he will say, "Yes" to Satan and his offer when Jesus said, "No:"

> "Then the devil taketh him up into
> An exceeding high mountain, and
> Sheweth him all the kingdoms of
> The world, and the glory of them;

And saith unto him, All these things
Will I give thee, if thou wilt fall down
And worship me. Then Jesus saith
Unto him, Get thee hence, Satan..."
Matthew 4: 8-10

Alright, what I would like to do at this point is introduce to you the name of the curse that exists on the Jewish Priests; yes, that's right, the curse has been given a name; and really, that shouldn't surprise you at all. In fact, do you remember the very, first topic that was covered in this book? It literally proved just how extremely meaningful names really are in the Holy Bible. Well, why do you think that point was to be established first? If you answered, "To make sure that the foundation for correctly understanding names is in place, so that I may know for an absolute fact that not only does God give names, but the names that He gives are, indeed, 100% significant, important, relative, meaningful, and sometimes even symbolic;" if you answered *exactly* like that, they you're doing good – really-good – in learning all about the antichrist's actual identity, and the Heavenly Father is most definitely proud of you. Why? Well, simply, because the honest-to-God truth of the matter is that the Lord really did name the curse, and the Curse of the Levitical Priests' name is "Leviathan."

Now, I must say, I definitely encountered some difficulty in understanding the reason for why God chose the name "Leviathan" to call the Curse of the Levitical Priests; and I had absolutely no idea that Leviathan and the Curse of the Levitical Priests are without question the beasts spoken of in Revelation 13 and 17 (Chapters 16, 19, and 20 also mention the curse.) I mean, I previously had read the Book of Revelation, and, was familiar with those two beasts mentioned in chapters 13 and 17, but trying to figure out the true significance and real reason for why God chose to name the Curse of the Levitical Priests, "Leviathan," was like trying to swim in a pool with no water; having said that, what He did reveal to me concerning those two beasts in those two chapters can be summed up in the following three undeniable truths:

1. The beasts in Revelation 13 and 17 are, in fact, the antichrist.
2. The beast described in Revelation 13 is the same beast as the beast in Revelation 17.
3. The beasts (as briefly stated earlier) in Revelation 13 and 17 are Leviathan, the curse of the Levitical Priests.

Those three factual points you just discovered really did come from God and they certainly are amazing, but as I said before, I did encounter incredible difficulty when I tried to understand why God chose to name the beast, "Leviathan." I really didn't understand; I really didn't, but I did know this: I knew – *without question* – that there was a genuine, legitimate reason for why He chose that specific name, because it is definitely specific; it can be found *nowhere* in The Holy Bible relating to anything *except* the antichrist; but having said that, I still couldn't figure out why He chose to give the antichrist the name of Leviathan until, of course, He once again opened up my eyes and undeservedly revealed the amazing answer to me.

You know, I must also say that I tried many different ways on my own to figure out the correct answer for why God chose the name "Leviathan" to call those two beasts in Revelation 13 and 17; I really did. I tried spelling Leviathan backwards (as if that would help); I tried assigning numbers to that name, but, unfortunately, whatever possible solution my mind could conceive, whatever idea I could possibly come up with in order to figure out the *real* reason for why God specifically chose and deliberately assigned the name, "Leviathan" to the antichrist, I always fell short in the end and was left sitting on the floor of my room all alone with nothing else but an overwhelming feeling of failure, disappointment, and defeat, not to mention the dreadful and loathsome silence that also was my unwanted companion; and then, suddenly, God finally opened my blinded eyes at last and showed me the answer that I had so desperately been seeking; it was right in front of me all the time, even looking and staring right back at me; yep, it sure was. Now, you go ahead and give it a try; take a look at the word, "Leviathan." What do *you* see? Do you see the answer, the correct answer for why God exclusively chose that name to call the two beasts in Revelation 13 and 17 who without question represent the Curse of the Levitical Priests, the antichrist? Do you see it? I'll give you a hint: The answer is located in the first four letters; yep, that's right, the very first four. Do you see it *now?* The correct answer is L-e-v-i, the Tribe of the Levites! That's right! *That's* why God chose that name! *That's* why he chose the name Leviathan! He specifically chose that name, "Leviathan," because the antichrist is a Levite, so God aptly named him – hence, "Leviathan." Wow! That's just incredible! It really is! Wow! But you know what? I should've known. I really should have. Why? Well, after all, the names that God chooses are *always* fitting and *always,* to say the least, extremely significant and full of meaning. *Right?*

So, The Holy Bible mentions Leviathan specifically only four times; it or he, depending on how you choose to view him (Leviathan, the cursed beast of the Levitical Priests or Leviathan, the cursed man who is the antichrist; either way, Leviathan is still the antichrist) does, however, have an entire chapter devoted just to him, giving intriguing clues and at times difficult to grasp characteristics and personality traits that make-up this diabolical, lofty, cursed beast known as the Leviathan; but before we read that truly fascinating chapter devoted entirely to him, let's first take a look at the other three holy sources of information; they are as follows:

> "So is this great and wide sea, wherein
> Are things creeping innumerable, both
> Small and great beasts. There go the
> Ships: there is that leviathan, whom
> Thou hast made to play therein."
> Psalm 104: 25-26

> "Thou brakest the heads of leviathan in
> Pieces, and gavest him to be meat to
> The people inhabiting the wilderness."
> Psalm 74: 14

"In that day the Lord with his sore and
Great and strong sword shall punish
Leviathan the piercing serpent, even
Leviathan that crooked serpent; and
He shall slay the dragon that is in the
Sea."
Isaiah 27: 1

The first scriptural reference places Leviathan in the sea; and that is true, but, unfortunately, I cannot comment on that right now, *maybe* later. The next scriptural reference, Psalm 74, has one little word that I have always felt holds all the clues, literally everything together that God so graciously revealed to me concerning the antichrist; it is the word, "heads," and it holds significant importance by proving without a shadow of any doubt that Leviathan is, in fact, none other than the antichrist. How does it do this? Well, first of all, one must be certain that in the Book of Revelation, the first beast in Chapter 13 and the beast in Chapter 17 are, indeed, the antichrist, and that they specifically possess heads, seven to be exact; these two, irrefutable truths *must* be understood first. Now, here's where that little word, the word, "heads" proves its immeasurable worth: In Psalm 74, Leviathan *also* has "heads," and *not* just one; it has more than one, exactly like the aforementioned beasts in Revelation 13 and 17; so, by this one little word being used in the plural tense and literally speaking of Leviathan at the same time, coupled with the other undeniable fact, the fact that the afore-mentioned beasts in Revelation 13 and 17 are, in fact, the antichrist, it can, therefore, be understandably and factually concluded that Leviathan is without question the antichrist. Additionally, because Leviathan is the anti-christ, it can also be correctly concluded that everywhere Leviathan is mentioned, the antichrist, too, is likewise being mentioned. So, as you can clearly see, that one little word, the word, "heads," is not only of great importance and of great, significant worth, but it absolutely holds fast and totally ties all the amazing clues pertaining to the antichrist's correct identity together.

The last scriptural passage speaks not only of the antichrist but Satan and the antichrist's evil buddy as well, calling the antichrist "the beast" and calling Satan by one of his many titles, "the dragon." It also, by the way, happens to be prophetic in nature, being that it directly speaks of "that day" when all three losers, the antichrist, his evil buddy, and Satan, are personally dealt with and totally disposed of by The Most High Himself. Here, you see for yourself:

"And the beast was taken, and with him
The false prophet that wrought miracles
Before him, with which he deceived them
That had received the mark of the beast,
And them that worshipped his image.
These both were cast alive into a lake of
Fire burning with brimstone."
Revelation 19: 20

"And I [the Apostle John] saw an angel
Come down from Heaven, having the
Key of the bottomless pit and a great
Chain in his hand. And he laid hold on
The dragon, that old serpent, which is
The Devil, and Satan, and bound him
A thousand years...and the devil that
Them was cast into the lake of fire
And brimstone, where the beast and
The false prophet are, and shall be
Tormented day and night for ever
And ever."
Revelation 20: 1-2; 10

Ok, we will now go ahead and take a look at that chapter
in The Holy Bible that is completely devoted to none

other than that cursed beast, Leviathan. I must first say, however, that I have often heard unnamed sources incorrectly state that Leviathan is nothing more than a dinosaur or possibly an alligator. Well, upon hearing this, for me to state that a partial smile did not begin to slowly form around the edges of my mouth would be just flat-out untruthful; it really would; and that I desire not, so I will just keep my mouth shut and continue to allow my fingers to do all of the talking. Having said that, here is your dinosaur – whoops, I mean, Leviathan (Sorry, I just had to do that.):

> "Canst thou draw out leviathan with an
> Hook? or his tongue with a cord which
> Thou lettest down? Canst thou put an
> Hook into his nose? or bore his jaw
> Through with a thorn? Will he make
> Many supplications unto thee? will he
> Speak soft words unto thee? will he
> Make a covenant with thee? wilt thou
> Take him for a servant for ever? Wilt
> Thou play with him as with a bird? or
> Wilt thou bind him for thy maidens?
> Shall the companions make a banquet
> Of him? shall they part him among the

Merchants? Canst thou fill his skin with
Barbed irons? or his head with fish spears?
Lay thine hand upon him, remember the
Battle, do no more. Behold, the hope of
Him is in vain; shall not one be cast down
Even at the sight of him? None is so fierce
That dare stir him up: who then is able to
Stand before me? Who hath prevented me,
That I should repay him? whatsoever is under
The whole heaven is mine. I will not conceal
His parts, nor his power, nor his comely
Proportion. Who can discover the face of
His garment? or who can come to him with
His double bridle? Who can open the doors
Of his face? His teeth are terrible round about.
His scales are his pride, shut up together as
With a close seal. One is so near to another,
That no air can come between them. They
Are joined one to another, they stick together,
That they cannot be sundered. By his neesings
A light doth shine, and his eyes are like the
Eyelids of the morning. Out of his mouth go
Burning lamps, and sparks of fire leap out.
Out of his nostrils goeth smoke, as out of a
Seething pot or caldron. His breath kindleth

Coals, and a flame goeth out of his mouth. In
His neck remaineth strength, and sorrow is
Turned into joy before him. The flakes of his
Flesh are joined together: they are firm in
Themselves; they cannot be moved. His heart
Is as firm as a stone; yea, as hard as a piece
Of the nether millstone. When he raiseth up
Himself, the mighty are afraid: by reason of
Breakings they purify themselves. The sword
Of him that layeth at him cannot hold: the
spear, the dart, nor the habergeon. He
Esteemeth iron as straw, and brass as rotten
Wood. The arrow cannot make him flee;
Slingstone are turned with him into stubble;
He laugheth at the shaking of a spear. Sharp
Stones are under him: he spreadeth sharp
Pointed things upon the mire. He maketh the
Deep to boil like a pot; he maketh the sea
Like a pot of ointment. He maketh a path to
Shine after him; one would think the deep
To be hoary. Upon earth there is not his like,
Who is made without fear. He beholdeth
All high things: he is a king over all the
Children of pride."
Job 41: 1-34

Alright, that chapter in God's word, I believe, is not only very interesting but absolutely loaded with special meaning and hidden clues that definitely give the reader one insightful look into the morbid and diabolical person of the antichrist. There are some clues, however, that I just cannot discuss or reveal at this point, because to do so would possibly jeopardize the revealing of the unmistakable identity of the antichrist. I can, however, discuss some verses, and the ones that I can are as follows:

> "Will he make a covenant with thee?"
> Verse 4

This statement in the form of a question is an obvious reference to the antichrist making a covenant with his hometown nation, the Nation of Israel. The Jews, having rejected their true messiah, Jesus Christ, will one day accept a fake one in the hellish form of the antichrist, and will, unfortunately, sign a seven year, peace covenant with him (This sad, prophetic truth was mentioned earlier back in a previous chapter and is found in Daniel 9: 27.).

The next verse:"Behold, the hope of him is in vain:

Shall not one be cast down even at
The sight of him?"
Verse 9

Now, among other things, the word "vain" here in this verse means to "…lie (i.e. deceive)."[18] Now, I've just got to ask: When was the last time you learned of a dinosaur or even an alligator having a hope (not to mention possessing the actual ability) to lie or deceive? (Obviously, the correct answer is, "Never." Dinosaurs and alligators do not possess the ability to have hope, lie, or deceive.) Secondly, do you think that the antichrist has the hope to lie or deceive (Of course he does; these two questions are rhetorical. I'm just simply making a point, and the point is this: Leviathan is *absolutely, without question* nothing other than the antichrist, and Leviathan also is certainly neither an alligator nor dinosaur.)?

As for the "sight of him," Leviathan will surely astonish and shock all who dare focus their eyes on him; the Apostle John puts it this way:

---

[18] Taken from *THE NEW STRONG'S EXHAUSTIVE CONCORDANCE OF THE BIBLE* by Strong, James, LL.D., . S.T.D., 63

"...and they that dwell on the earth shall
Wonder, whose names were not written
In the book of life from the foundation of
The world, when they behold the beast
[the antichrist]."
Revelation 17: 8

The next verse:"His heart is as firm as a stone; yea, as
Hard as a piece of the nether millstone."
Verse 24

Yes, the antichrist's heart will certainly be hard; it will also
be very cold; here, you take a look for yourself:

"And the Lord said unto me [Zechariah],
Take unto thee yet the instruments of
A foolish shepherd. For, lo, I will raise
Up a shepherd in the land [Israel], which
Shall not visit those that be cut off,
Neither shall seek the young one, nor
Heal that is broken, nor feed that
Standeth still: but he shall eat the
Flesh of the fat, and tear their claws
In pieces."
Zechariah 11: 15-16

The last verse:"He [the antichrist] beholdeth all high
Things: he is a king over all the children
Of pride."
Verse 34

Whoa! Now, this verse is *so* telling! Without a doubt, this
verse out of all the other 33 verses is clearly the most
important and the most insightful one; it actually contains three of the four clues given thus far; yes, it certainly
does. Let's go ahead and take a closer look at it right now.

"He beholdeth all high things" is a reference to the antichrist one day being a high priest; it also speaks of his
disgusting tendency to be completely full of himself.

"He is a king" speaks of the antichrist being chosen one
day by the Nation of Israel to be – what else—their king
(The scriptural references supporting and, more importantly, proving this factual, forthcoming occurrence were
given in an earlier chapter; but guess what? You were
also just given another scriptural reference; it's the one
where God calls the antichrist a "foolish shepherd," saying,
"For, lo, I will raise up a shepherd in the land [Israel;
Zechariah 11: 15]…"

"He is a king over all the children of pride" speaks volumes; yes, it does; it *absolutely does;* it literally cements even further the validity and soundness of the very first clue that was given, "Pride is His Best Friend." God's word states here that prideful people will one day accept, honor, and respect the antichrist as their king – and this means people of all races – but in doing so, he will become their diabolical and corrupt father, and they will, in turn, become his no-good and foolish children (just like how God does those that accept Him and make Him their God) with pride most definitely being the catalyst to all of this.

Ok, right now, we're going to take a look at a very interesting and informative passage, a passage where Leviathan is actually addressed by none other than God Himself. Yep, that's right, God definitely does address Leviathan, but that really ought not to surprise you too much because, as we have already seen in some previous verses, God does at times choose to personally address certain individuals. Here, now, is that passage;

> "But ye are they that forsake the Lord,
> That forget my holy mountain, that
> Prepare a table for that troop, and

That furnish the drink offering unto
That number. Therefore will I number
You to the sword, and ye shall all bow
Down to the slaughter: because when
I called, ye did not answer; when I spake,
Ye did not hear; but did evil before mine
Eyes, and did not choose that wherein
I delighted not. Therefore thus saith
The Lord God, Behold, my servants
Shall eat, but ye shall be hungry: behold,
My servants shall drink, but ye shall be
Thirsty: behold, my servants shall rejoice,
But ye shall be ashamed: Behold, my
Servants shall sing for joy of heart, but ye
Shall cry for sorrow of heart, and shall
Howl for vexation of spirit. And ye shall
Leave your name for a curse unto my
Chosen: for the Lord God shall slay thee..."
Isaiah 65: 11-15

Boy, God really starts off with a bang on this passage. The very first sentence is a clue to the identity of the antichrist, and therefore, no comment at this time will be given (*Surely,* you wouldn't want to find out who the antichrist is right *now,* would you?). God goes on to say that the antichrist will "prepare a table for that troop." The antichrist will most certainly do just that when he gathers a huge troop, a huge army in a fool hearted attempt to defeat God; but just as you read those earlier verses that spoke of the antichrist's demise, he certainly will come up very short and will be completely humiliated as well as defeated, both he and his inept and laughable troop. God then says that the antichrist will "furnish the drink offering unto that number." Well, regarding this part of the passage, first you have to understand that a drink offering was a part of worship; and being that the antichrist will one day be a high priest, it's no wonder that God declares that the antichrist will, in fact, use a priestly function in worship (which is the second point). "Worship?" someone might ask. Yes, worship. Clearly, God is saying that He totally disapproves of worship being directed to "that number." What number is God referring to? "That number" would be the antichrist's number or the number of his name, the same number that will one day be placed on people's (the people that will choose to worship the antichrist) foreheads or right hands, the same number that will one day bring the antichrist the glory (because he's so full of himself and such a glory monger) that he will so desperately seek, and the same, exact number that has already been prophetically spoken of by God and through the Apostle John's writing hand to

serve as a warning to the entirety of mankind of the horrible and idolatrous events that will one day center around
"that number" of the antichrist. Here, you see for yourself:

> "And he [the antichrist's helper] causeth
> All, both small and great, rich and poor,
> Free and bond, to receive a mark in their
> Right hand, or in their foreheads: and that
> No man might buy or sell, save he that had
> The mark, or the name of the beast [the
> Antichrist], or the number of his name.
> Here is wisdom. Let him that hath
> Understanding count the number of the
> Beast: for it is a number of a man; and
> His number is Six hundred three score
> And six [666]."
> Revelation 13: 16-18

> "And the first [angel] went, and poured
> Out his vial upon the earth; and there fell
> A noisome and grievous sore upon the
> Men which had the mark of the beast
> [the antichrist], and upon them which
> Worshipped his image."
> Revelation 16: 2

Next, we come to the latter part of the passage where God is speaking directly to the antichrist, and where it is absolutely loaded with very interesting information concerning the antichrist. God specifically and clearly states that this extremely prideful man of Jewish descent belonging to the Tribe of Levi will one day leave his name "for a curse." Wow! Now, that's just amazing! It certainly also qualifies as a juicy tidbit, I might add. God's words actually acknowledge that the man behind the title of a Jewish High Priest will one day have his name changed due to him leaving and forsaking God and willfully turning into – actually taking on and becoming – Leviathan, the Curse of the Levitical Priests. Wow, how much more clearer does it have to be in order to see and admit that a curse has absolutely been placed on the Levitical Priests in the dreaded and evil form of Leviathan? How much more undeniable evidence is needed? Wow! God is *so* amazing, *so* awesome in power and mighty in strength; no one can compare to Him, and the same goes for His word.

As you discovered earlier, when one (or even an entire nation) does not humble themselves and actually refuses to confess their willful, deliberate sin, that's when problems arise; and before they know it, because of their unconfessed sin, there certainly is a wage to be paid; and when there is a sin-wage, if you will, due, well, let's just say that's when one really ought to get down on their knees, repent of their prideful, obstinate sin, and get right with the Heavenly Father.

At this point, four of five clues plus two additional topics, one being the Levitical Curse, have all been revealed. Do you have a person of interest as to who could possibly be the antichrist? Well, do you feel that it would help if we were to review the clues? Ok, let's review the clues that have been given so far:

1. The antichrist will be extremely prideful.
2. The antichrist's "deadly wound" will actually be a stroke.
3. The antichrist will be of Jewish descent.
4. The antichrist will one day be a Levitical High Priest.

HIS BIRTHDAY CAKE IS ENORMOUS

I KNOW, RIGHT NOW YOU'RE PROBABLY THINKING or maybe even have already said out loud, "What...birthday cake? Huh?" Well, please be rest assured that there are, indeed, reasons for why that title says what it says, as you will no doubt discover soon enough. So, having said that, do you still celebrate your birthday? At least *some of us* still celebrate our own birthday, *right?* Well, whether we are celebrating our own special day when for the very first time we actually took a breath of fresh air into our brand new, little lungs or we're just simply celebrating someone else's, there probably are a few, good friends and family members with us, enjoying each other's company, talking, laughing, and having a good time. Most likely, a gift or two are sitting on top of the dining room table, wrapped ever so neatly with bright, attractive colors; but the one, single thing that we all expect to see and – let's be honest

– eagerly want to taste, is a yummy looking birthday cake and *especially* if it's one made with ice cream.

Well, I must say, God didn't reveal everything to me about the antichrist (and this includes whether or not he prefers a regular, baked cake versus a scrumptious and delightfully tasteful ice cream one like myself.), only enough to undeniably prove to me – and hopefully everyone else – that he *really* is the Lofty Lunatic of Lucifer, the Son of Perdition, that Wicked, Man of Sin; but, having said all that, one of the things that God *did* reveal to me is the antichrist's approximate age, and, boy, let me tell you, for his upcoming birthday, he'll *definitely* need to order an enormous cake – XXL even; yep, he sure will. Why? Well, this way, he can make absolute certain that there will be enough room for all those candles representing his true age to be strategically placed on top.

Alright, people have different ideas and theories concerning the antichrist's age. The top three, prevailing theories concerning the antichrist's age are what we will now take a look at; but before we go any further, let's title this part of the chapter, "Exhibit A: The Antichrist's Age." This part of the chapter is being titled because although it will now be examined, we will eventually abandon it but return at a later time and complete our examination. Also, please note that other, forthcoming parts located within this chapter will, too, be given a corresponding title; this way, they'll be easy to recall. Ok, with that said, here, now, are the three prevailing theories that some people actually believe are true and even outwardly state, defend, and support:

1. The antichrist is an adult right now, somewhere on Planet Earth, desperately concealing his true identity in a conscious effort to not stand out in any way while working in some sort of political or military setting amongst others, quietly biding his allotted time and blending in perfectly with an unsuspecting society as he discreetly waits for his much anticipated opportunity to deviously but yet confidently come forth and reveal himself as God to all people of every tongue and every nation.

2. The antichrist is alive here on Planet Earth but is a young boy or possibly even younger, surrounded by his modern family and experiencing a normal childhood free of any major troubles. He also, at this point in his young life, may not even know that he is the one who, as it was mentioned previously, will one day accept Satan's offer to become

the Curse of the Levitical Priests, Leviathan, the antichrist.

3. The antichrist is not on Planet Earth, because he has not yet been born.

Ok, go ahead and take, if you will, a good, hard look at those three actual theories, because we are now going to leave this exhibit, Exhibit A, and get into another fascinating topic that's relative to the forthcoming and final clue regarding the exact identity of the antichrist.

All the books of the Holy Bible are priceless and irreplaceable, to say the least. In the Book of Revelation, because its subject matter primarily revolves around the incredible events during and after the time of the Tribulation (a period of seven years after the Lord Jesus returns close to Planet Earth and gathers every one of His children – none, by the way, that by *choice* are not His – in what is commonly referred to as, "the Rapture"), it, therefore, contains much information not just about the Tribulation, but it also reveals astounding, prophetic truths concerning the antichrist as well. Now, before we go any further, it should be noted that the Apostle John is the one who physically wrote the Book of Revelation after he received a shocking, unexpected but very welcomed visit from the

Lord Jesus who then gave him one miraculous and revelatory vision – hence, "the Book of Revelation."

Now, a *very, very* important question: When did the
Apostle John write the Book of Revelation? Please do
not make any mistake about it; this question is of *extreme*
importance, and even happens to be one of the biggest
clues within this very book; yes, it certainly is (This section of discussion, by the way, is titled, "Exhibit B: When
the Book of Revelation was Written."). Well, generally
speaking and by most accounts, the Book of Revelation
was written about 60 years after the death of the Savior
of the World, Jesus Christ; so, that would make the date
roughly between A.D. 90 and 100; some sources, I must
say, date the book even earlier than this; but that's Ok;
here's what Dr. Willmington has to say regarding the year
that the book was written:

> "I John, who also am your brother,
> And companion in tribulation, and
> In the kingdom and patience of Jesus
> Christ, was in the isle that is called Pat-
> Mos, for the word of God, and for the
> Testimony of Jesus Christ.
> John now explains why he was on the

> Isle. He was exiled there from about
> A.D. 86 to 96."[19]

So, there we have it. The Book of Revelation was written somewhere around 60 years – possibly even earlier – after the Lord Jesus died for your sins and mine. Now, at this time, what I'd like to say is this: Knowing the exact date when John wrote the Book of Revelation is really not necessary, and it is also not relative to the provability of anything in this entire book, including the fifth and final major clue that you will soon receive while reading this very page. What *is* necessary and important, however, is that there would be an understanding that somewhere between the years of A.D. 50 to 100, the Book of Revelation was written; that is what's important.

Alright, you will now be given a setting, a mental environment, if you will, to think about and picture in your mind. Once the setting is finished, three questions and even some comments regarding that setting will follow; this section, by the way, is titled, "Exhibit C: The Office Setting," and as it has been the case with the last section, please try to

---

[19] Dr. H.L. Willmington, *"Willmington's Guide to the Bible"* (Wheaton: Tyndale House Publishers Inc, 1984), 539

remember this setting, its valid points, comments as well as all the answers made from the forthcoming questions, because they, too, will be later referenced. Ok? Alright, here goes:

Eleven years ago, that would be the year of 2009, you were working as an administrative assistant. You were known for possessing the ability to take dictation, a skill in which you literally write down every word that is spoken by another person. The person speaking is called the dictator. Anyway, one day you were called into the office of your boss to take dictation for him. Your boss's name is Mr. Eaton. Before he started to speak, he politely reminded you to write down every word that he spoke. This is what he told you eleven years ago, and this is exactly what you wrote:

> "We worked for that company for a
> Long time. It was alive and running,
> And is not alive and running today,
> But shall, however, rise up and run
> Again."

Now, let's leave Mr. Eaton's office and come back to reality, because there are a few questions that need to be asked;

here's the first one: Eleven years ago in the year 2009 when you wrote exactly what Mr. Eaton said, was the company alive? The correct answer is, "No." This means that the company existed, had it's life, if you will, and was alive *prior* to eleven years ago, 2009; *that* is the correct and *only* correct conclusion.

Ok, next question: Eleven years ago in the year 2009 when you wrote what Mr. Eaton spoke to you, was the company dead or alive? The correct answer is, "dead." This means that the company had already lived its life but died some time before eleven years ago, 2009; *that* is the correct and *only* correct conclusion.

Ok, last question: Eleven years ago in the year 2009 when you wrote what Mr. Eaton spoke to you, according to him, will the company rise and run again? The correct answer is, "Yes." This means that some time after eleven years ago, after the year 2009, the company will, once again, rises and run; *that* is the correct and *only* correct conclusion.

Alright, it's now time for some shocking, eye-opening, incredible truths – truths that have never been revealed, and truths that are now only being revealed because of the Lord Jesus Himself – that are probably going to blow the socks right off your feet, make your hair stand straight up no matter how curly it may be, and open your mouth so wide that all you'll be able to see is the outside of your upper lip; and as if that wasn't overwhelming enough, it is also now time for all three exhibits to be brought back and examined so that their incredible relativity and importance will not only be tied together with the fifth and final clue, but that they might also be thoroughly explained; again, the fifth and final clue regarding the absolute identity of the antichrist will soon be revealed, and all that starts right now with these three verses (Please note that "the angel" is the angel that I spoke of earlier, the one that helped John correctly understand the vision.):

> "And the angel said unto me [John],
> Wherefore didst thou marvel? I will
> Tell thee the mystery...of the beast...
> The beast that thou sawest was, and is
> Not; and shall ascend out of the bottomless
> Pit, and go into perdition: and they that
> Dwell on the earth shall wonder, whose
> Names were not written in the book of
> Life from the foundation of the world,
> When they behold the beast that was,

And is not, and yet is."
Revelation 17: 7-8

"And the beast that was, and is not…and
Goeth into perdition."
Revelation 17: 11

Ok, here it is, here's the fifth and final clue regarding the identity of the antichrist: The reason why his birthday cake needs to be so enormous, the reason why all the prevailing theories regarding his age (examined earlier in Exhibit A) are incorrect (That's right; *all* of them are wrong, *not one* is right.), the reason why it's *so* necessary and important to understand when the Book of Revelation was written (examined earlier in Exhibit B), the reason why understanding "Exhibit C: The Office Setting" is *so* important, is because the antichrist, the Curse of the Levitical Priests, Leviathan, is dead; *he is dead.* Yes, that's right. The antichrist is now dead and not living; he is *absolutely, positively dead;* that's the fifth and final clue.

Now, I do think an apology from me is in order; yes, I do. Why? Well, in order to keep you in all the suspense I possibly could, I kinda implied that the antichrist *perhaps* might be alive and is definitely not what the scriptures clearly say he is – that he is, in fact, dead. So, with that, I'm sorry. My sole intention was -- and still is – to keep you on the edge of your seat.

Alright, at this time, verse eight (one of the last, three verses you just read) will now be examined in a much greater detail, revealing God-given, Spirit-filled truths never before seen or heard; and while all three exhibits – Exhibits A, B, and C – from time to time will be mentioned, please don't forget that "Exhibit A: The Antichrist's Age" and "Exhibit C: The Office Setting" will be examined in a much greater detail as well; I have no doubt that they even will reveal more God-given, Spirit-filled truths as well. As for "Exhibit B: When the Book of Revelation was Written," it has already been established and, more importantly, proven.

Ok, just think of how many people – me included – and how many times verse eight as well as those two other verses regarding the antichrist's age, the ones we just took a look at (Revelation 17: 7-8; 11), were not only read and, most likely, studied exhaustively but were never correctly understood, never properly applied and connected to the antichrist's age the way that they are meant to be. Well, thanks to God the exact meanings of those three verses are now fully known, and can finally be understood correctly; but before we go any further, there are two truths that should quickly be stated, and they are as follows: Verse eleven is just a repeat of verse seven (one), and, as previously mentioned, one must completely understand that the beast here in Revelation 17 is, in fact, the antichrist (two); once those two truths are understood, then forward progress is not only on track but, most importantly, correctly on. So, with that said, let's go ahead and begin examining verse eight; it states that the beast (the antichrist):

> "was, and is not; and shall ascend out of
> The bottomless pit..."

Now, this part of verse eight is absolutely loaded with pertinent information, so much that just knowing where to begin is somewhat difficult; but the foundation should always be laid first, so let's go there. We'll start with the verbs of verse eight; they are "was," "is not," and "shall ascend." Those verbs all by themselves are somewhat difficult to understand; they really are; that's because one, single, very important word is missing, and in order for you to correct understand just what verse eight is actually saying, that one, very important word is definitely needed. So, which all-important word do I speak of? Well, the word that I right now speak of and that is also 100% needed in order to correctly understand just what verse eight is truly saying is the word, "alive." So, having said that, please, if you will, take that very important word and place it after the verbs "was," "is not," and "shall." Now, read the verse. What does it say? Does it make sense now? It should, and it should look just like this:

> "…[the antichrist that] was [alive],
> And is not [alive]; and shall ascend
> [alive] out of the bottomless pit…"

Do you see the true meaning now? Do you understand what this verse is *really* saying in regards to the antichrist's age? Do you? This verse is unquestionably telling us that at some point in the past, the antichrist was alive – *he was alive,* meaning he *already lived his life* and is now *not* alive, meaning he *already has died* and is now not living anymore but will eventually ascend out of the bottomless pit alive (He will ascend out of the bottomless pit alive where he currently is dead right now.); *this* is what verse is saying; *this* is the *true and only meaning* of verse eight; and this is what verse eight totally speaks of.

Please understand, however, that the word, "alive" is not in any way, shape, or form being added to God's word; no, it is not. The truth of the matter is that it is already part of the true meaning and actual definition of verse eight, but because the verse was written so unusually, it was, therefore, difficult to grasp, difficult to thoroughly understand and, consequently, caused me to be in need of just a little bit of help from above from my heavenly Father. Hey, trust me, I can hardly tie my shoes. If the good Lord didn't open these once blinded eyes of mine and reveal verse's eight's -- as well as everything else's -- true meaning, I'd *still* be lost, *still* be stuck in the mud. Let this be known and known to all: It's all because of God that I understand what He personally revealed to me. Believe me; I am *well* aware of what I can do on my own and in my own strength:

> "for without me [my God and Savior,
> The Lord Jesus] ye [I, Timothy] can
> Do nothing."
> John 15: 5

Ok, the next point that we will now look at revolves around the antichrist's rise from his fiery place of torment. Here, now, is the corresponding verse:

"...and [the antichrist] shall ascend
Out of the bottomless pit."

The fact that the antichrist will one day experience an actual resurrection and leave the bottomless pit where he is located right now has been seen in the scriptures thus far, but the first three words of the above verse, "and shall ascend," just have not received their due diligence. So, let's not prolong giving them their just due anymore; let's go ahead and focus in on them right now; they are, by the way, *truly* a key part of the verse. The very meaning of these three words is right before your eyes. God's word is acknowledging and proving at the same time that the antichrist's resurrection will take place *first* before he's allowed to do anything else; he then will be allowed to leave the bottomless pit and show himself – be revealed – to the people of the world – hence, he "...shall ascend..." You see, the truth of the matter is not that he will eventually experience a resurrection after already being revealed; no, that is *completely* false and *absolutely* not true. What *is* true is that he will experience his own, personal resurrection when he is allowed to leave the bottomless pit where he currently resides; *that's* when his resurrection takes place; it takes place *first*.

The final point of verse eight that we will now look at more closely is the part saying, "...and go into perdition." First, this part of the verse speaks of the antichrist returning back into Hell once he is totally humiliated and defeated in battle by God (This one day event has already been discussed and proven at an earlier time.); that's what it means by perdition. Now, what's so strikingly intriguing about this one word "perdition," is that the Apostle Paul actually referred to the antichrist with this very, same, exact word; yep, he sure did. Here's the proof:

> "...and that man of sin be revealed, the Son of perdition;"
> 2 Thessalonians 2: 3

Simply put: God's word is just amazing. More detailed: Clearly, both of these verses, verse eight in Revelation 17 and here in 2 Thessalonians speak of that Lofty Lunatic of Lucifer, the "...son of perdition;"

Alright, so, do you remember "Exhibit C: The Office Setting?" Well, at this time, I'd like to go ahead and bring that back just one more time, so that we can look at verse eight through the magnifying glass, if you will, of Exhibit C. Sound good? Yeah, I think so too. Here we go!

If you recall, Exhibit C was basically a story of you as an administrative assistant. You were called to your boss's office to take dictation. Well, you may have noticed that what you wrote down mirrored verse eight, the verse that says the antichrist "was [alive], is not [alive], and shall ascend [alive]…" The setting was also very similar to that of what the Apostle John experienced. In John's vision regarding verse eight, there are three main people; they are the antichrist, the angel, and the Apostle John; and in Exhibit C, there are also three main subjects; they are you, the boss, and the company. So, in an effort to make things easy to understand in the forthcoming outline, the angel who represents your boss will have "the angel" in parentheses next to the words, "your boss," the antichrist who represents the company will have "the antichrist" in parentheses next to the company, and John who represents you will have "you" in parentheses next to John. Alright? Hopefully, by doing it this way, we'll get even a better understanding. Here, now, is the outline:

1. The company (the antichrist) was alive and lived prior to . 2009 (A.D. 100).
2. The company (the antichrist) died previous to 2009 (A.D.. 100).

3. You (John) writing the message from your boss (the angel) in 2009 (A.D. 100) does in no way affect the company's (the antichrist) age at all. Regardless of you (John) writing this message back in 2009 (A.D. 100), it makes no difference and has absolutely no impact or affect on the life or death of the company (the antichrist). The company (the antichrist) still lived and died prior to the year of 2009 (A.D. 100) regardless of the amount of years that have since passed.

Hopefully, if you hadn't seen it before, you can now see for yourself that by comparing Exhibit C with the vision of John, *none* of the facts were altered or affected in *any* way. The truth of the matter is that the antichrist has already lived and died way before the Book of Revelation was written. Make no mistake about it: The antichrist is *dead,* and dead because he has *already lived* his life some time before A.D. 100. Plus, we can also irrefutably conclude that since the Book of Revelation was written some time before A.D. 100, then the antichrist without question lived and died at the minimum of 1900 years ago – yep, 1900 years! Wow! That's incredible! Well someone might ask, "So, the antichrist is at least 2000 years old?" Yes, as a matter of fact, he is; he certainly is; and it's no wonder why the scriptures plainly tell us that the antichrist will one day be the only one on Planet Earth with the amazing ability to understand puzzles or riddles that will be completely unsolvable to everyone else:

> "a king [the antichrist] of fierce
> Countenance, and understanding
> Dark sentences, shall stand up."
> Daniel 8: 23

The wisdom, albeit totally corrupt and full of wickedness that the antichrist will possess just from being at the minimum of 2000 years old will no doubt be astounding. As for his age, well, now, let's just say that's certainly the case for him truly having a need not just for an enormous birthday cake, but, more specifically, one big enough to showcase – at the very least – 2000 lighted candles.

Well, thanks to God there's much, much more to be revealed. More important and more shocking facts are on the way, ones that will, once again, cause your socks to be blown right off of your feet, make your hair stand straight up no matter how curly it may be, and open your mouth so wide that all you'll be able to see is the outside of your upper lip; yep, I'm serious; they're on their way!

So, grab a hold of that chair of yours, put your socks back on, and fix your upper lip, because this exhilarating and thrilling ride has only just begun!

Next up: "Exhibit A: The Antichrist's Age"

If you remember, Exhibit A detailed the three, prevailing theories that people embrace regarding not just the antichrist's age, but also his location and environment. However, as you learned earlier from the scriptures, the antichrist -- even this very second – is neither alive nor unborn. In fact, he has *already* lived his life and is currently dead. Furthermore, God's word also states that he, too, will experience a resurrection (just like the Lord Jesus did) upon his very arrival and introduction to every living thing on Planet Earth and absolutely not some time later after his presence is already made public or, for that matter, after a bullet strikes his head. This is why the scriptures actually imply that *upon arriving,* upon the people of the world seeing him *for the very first time,* they are completely in awe, completely shocked, and in complete and total amazement; that, without question, is the scriptures implication. In effect, here's what the scriptures actually say regarding all the people of the world's actions and statements when, *for the very first time* and with their very own eyeballs, they gaze upon the Curse of the Levitical Priests, the antichrist:

> "and they [the people] worshipped the
> Beast [the antichrist], saying Who is like
> Unto the beast? Who is able to make
> War with him?
> Revelation 13: 4

Excuse me, please allow me to step in here for just a second; this verse demands a comment. Question: Why do you think the people of the world will say, "Who is like unto the beast? Who is able to make war with him?" when they see him for the very first time (After all that has been revealed to you, you definitely should know this answer.)? The answer to their first question ("Who is like unto the beast?"): Well, without revealing too much, who do you know actually returns from the dead? Who do you know after being dead for over *2000 years* literally comes back to life and is standing before your very eyes? Well?

The answer to their last question ("Who is able to make war with him?"): How can they "...make war with him" and kill him who has literally triumphed over death? How can they "...make war with him" and kill him who has by his own incredible power (This is one of the lies that the people of the world will believe.) already defeated death and is now actually alive before your very eyes – talking, walking, looking around, moving their head and their body? How can they kill someone that has *already died?* He will just come back again! How can they who haven't died yet, whose body is still of the physical nature, "...make war with him" and kill him whose body is now of the *spiritual* nature? How are they, being of the physical realm, able to kill someone who is of the spiritual realm? How are they going to kill him? What do they have, and what are they going to use to "...make war with him" and kill him who has a spiritual body? How are they going to do that? How are they going to defeat him? *How can they?* The fact of the matter is that it's *totally impossible* for them to defeat him who has a spiritual body, and that is why they will one day say, "Who is like unto the beast? Who is able to make war with him?" when they see him for the very, first time.

See, this is why even God says Himself that the anti-christ will look so scary, so imposing, so amazing and truly unbelievable that the people of the world will just about fall to the ground in their absolute stunning terror of shock and disbelief. Man, can you believe *that?* Boy, he is going to look so mind blowing! Yes, God, by the way, really did say that, and here, now, is the proof:

> "shall not one be cast down even at the sight of him?"
> Job 41: 9

One word: Wow. Continuing, now, are the rest of the supporting references regarding the people of the world's immediate reactions when they look upon the antichrist for the very, first time:

> "The beast [the antichrist] that thou
> Sawest was, and is not; and shall ascend
> Out of the bottomless pit; and they that
> Dwell on the earth shall wonder...when
> They behold [when for the very, first time
> They see] the beast that was, and is not,
> And yet is."
> Revelation 17: 8

> "...and all the world wondered after the beast
> [the antichrist]."
> Revelation 13: 3

> "And all that dwell upon the earth shall

Worship him [the antichrist], whose names
Are not written in the book of life of the
Slain from foundation of the world."
Revelation 13: 8

So, as you just witnessed for yourself, all three of the prevailing theories Exhibit A speaks of are totally incorrect.

Well, that's pretty much it for the fifth and final clue, "His Birthday Cake is Enormous." It's probably fair to say that if you didn't have a clue as to what the true meaning of that title is when you first read it, you definitely know now. Personally, next to the awesome clue, "His Deadly Wound," this one, here, seemed to be more of a surprise.

So, here it is; here is the moment that you probably have been waiting for and even felt that it couldn't come soon enough. Now, *right now,* is your last, official chance to make a guess at who could possibly be the antichrist; yep, it sure is. It's your last chance, because in the next chapter, the antichrist's identity will finally be revealed.

You know, we've certainly come a long way, and hopefully, you have been thrilled at times and also amazed while you discovered a lot of God's amazing, hidden meanings and glorious truths regarding the unmistakable identity of the antichrist (All praise and glory, by the way, belongs to God for revealing those wonderful, undeserved truths to me.). So, with that said, are you now ready to make your last, official guess? Well, hold on; it probably would be best if we were to review all of those incredible, God-given, Holy Ghost-inspired clues just one last time. Shall we? Ok, here they are:

1. The antichrist will be extremely prideful.
2. The antichrist's deadly wound *was* a stroke.
3. The antichrist *is* of Jewish descent.
4. The antichrist *was and again will be* a High Priest.
5. The antichrist is actually dead *right now* and has been for a very long time.

And the Loser is...

Next to the Devil, the antichrist has to be the biggest loser. He was a loser from the beginning when he was first on Planet Earth the first time, he's a loser today as he lays in the bottomless pit of Hell, literally suffering in torment and burning like an old, seasoned oak log this very second as you read these very words, and he will *still* be a complete and total loser when he is resurrected from the bottomless pit and returns for a second time back to Planet Earth; *this* is the man – or loser, sorry – behind the title, "the antichrist," a definite loser that is just a complete and utter, no-good, failure of a person, priest, and even antichrist. Why do I say that? Well, if he truly is as good as God (of which I'm positive he certainly thinks so), then why is he right now burning in Hell? If he truly is as good, why will he receive the whooping of his life and, once again, for the *second* and final time, be totally humiliated and completely destroyed when he meets God in battle? Why, I say, why? No, the cold, hard truth of the matter is this: The antichrist is not a winner; he's not cool, and he's definitely not as good as God. The antichrist is, however, a joke. He's a foolish traitor, an absolute disgrace, a total wannabe, and without question a complete and utter loser.

Well, before I actually unveil just who the antichrist actually is, I thought it would be a good idea if I were to give you a couple more, final clues that point directly to his true identity; but don't worry; they're not nearly as long as the other five. In fact, each clue only consists of a small amount of words, and there are just two of them. Plus, after the clues are given and the antichrist is revealed, then we'll go over each one quickly, and I'll show you just how they point directly to the identity of the antichrist. Ok? Alright, here goes:

Clue #1: Yale University

Clue #2: lofty

So, do those two clues help? Do you think you know who the antichrist is *now?* Perhaps you do know who the antichrist is and have already solved one of the greatest mysteries of mankind, a mystery, certainly, like no other, and one that for the last 2000 years has remained completely intact and absolutely impossible to crack, while effortlessly escaping the sharp intellect of a great host of countless scholars, theologians, and men and women of God. Therefore, let it be known: If you really do know who the antichrist is and have solved this tremendous, very old mystery, then congratulations is in order. Congratulations! If, however, you still are not sure whether you have the right man or not, well, I'm afraid that time is, indeed, up; so, with that said, are you now ready to finally find out the identity of the antichrist? Ok, here we go: The biggest failure of mankind as well as the biggest loser of mankind is none other than Eli. Yes, Eli. You know, Eli, the high priest spoken of in the first Book of Samuel who also judged the Nation of Israel for forty years and who is mostly known for failing as a father; yeah, *that* Eli, *that* one. *He's* the antichrist; *he's* the one who is currently being held captive and burning in the Bottomless Pit of Hell; he's the one who in times past initially died of an actual stroke, the one who will one day be satanically resurrected and allowed to return back to earth so that he may completely deceive countless numbers of people, and the one who is overflowing with an abundance of pride, haughtiness, loftiness, arrogance, egotism, pomp, and the false and ridiculous belief of him possessing personal superiority over literally everyone else including God. Eli's also the one who has, until now, successfully escaped positive identification for the past 2000 years, the one who long ago said "Yes" to Satan's idolatrous offer to one day rule over most of the world's population, the one who will one day reign gloriously (albeit diabolically) as king, and the one who will one day again suffer a deadly wound from God and be thoroughly humiliated as well as destroyed once and for all with absolutely, positively *no* chance of ever experiencing another resurrection of any kind whatsoever; *he* is that wicked "...man of sin..." spoken of in the scriptures, *he* is that evil "...son of perdition..." written in The Holy Bible, *he* is the antichrist.

So, how do you feel? Are you shocked that Eli is the antichrist? Is Eli the one that you had in your mind, the man you suspected? Was he even one of your suspects? Well, certainly, when God so graciously revealed to me that Eli really is the antichrist, I definitely was shocked. I, to put it mildly, was *very* surprised. I thought, "Wow, it is *really him?* Is he *really* the antichrist? As I said earlier, I always thought of Eli as just a priest and father (no doubt like the rest of the world does), a priest who served God to the best of his ability and, generally speaking, in a good and acceptable way, and a loving father who, unfortunately, failed in the raising of his two sons who served alongside of him also as priests. To me, those were pretty much the extent of my thoughts and feelings I had towards Eli and how I saw him as a whole; they really were. I had absolutely *no idea* that it is *he* who will one day be the loser who will become the antichrist, just as much as I had no idea that God would one day actually reveal to *me* (of all people) the exact identity of the antichrist. Needless to say, Eli never showed up on my antichrist radar, no "ping" was ever heard from my antichrist tower, and, surely, a "beep" never, *ever* sounded from my antichrist detector.

Well, now that Eli has been revealed as the antichrist, the Curse of the Levitical Priests, let's go ahead and take a look at those two, quick clues that were given earlier:

Clue #1: Yale University – This happens to be a very good clue and, it, too, points directly at Eli. How does it? Well, if you are a student at Yale or have already graduated, you are officially titled an "Eli." Yeah, can u believe that? It's the truth, and it's also quite interesting.

Clue #2: lofty – Now, to me this clue certainly is the best one. Why? Well, it's the best clue because "lofty" is the actual meaning of the antichrist's name; yep, that's right. Eli's name literally means "lofty."[20] Wow, can you believe *that*? Isn't that just *amazing?* The scriptures adamantly tell us that the antichrist will, indeed, be prideful, and now it's divulged that the very meaning of Eli's name is "lofty." I bet someone, somewhere is saying this in a higher than normal pitch with their eyes wide open right now: "*What is the meaning of Eli's actual name? No way! Lofty?*" My response: "Yep, lofty." Wow! Now, that's just incredible! It really is! Plus, don't forget: The very, first clue given in this book regarding the identity of the antichrist was that he would be lofty or full of pride, remember? See, I told you. I told you that *all* of the names that God gives are 100%, absolutely significant and hold great, noteworthy meaning. See, I told you!

By the way, you may have noticed that at times within this book whenever the antichrist was specifically being mentioned, he was referred to as, "the Lofty Lunatic of Lucifer." That was done on purpose; it was done in an effort to point the reader Eli's way so that they might

---

[20] Taken from *THE NEW STRONG'S EXHAUSTIVE CONCORDANCE OF THE BIBLE* by Strong, James,. LL.D., S.T.D., 106

possibly pick up on the subtle hint of Eli literally being the man whom they desperately seek to positively identify as the antichrist; and due to names in God's word being extremely important and significant, it was also done to prepare the reader for the reality of the antichrist's name actually being one that, too, totally describes him to the proverbial "T." So, needless to say, one would certainly be correct in saying that calling the antichrist "the Lofty Lunatic of Lucifer" was definitely an suggestive attempt to help clue the reader and, at the same time, put those antichrist cross hairs squarely on Eli.

Alright, now that the marvelous mystery regarding the antichrist's true identity has been factually, biblically, and historically solved and a person – the *only* person – has been positively identified, namely Eli, what I'd like to do right now is go ahead and reveal some very interesting facts pertaining to Eli that I just could not reveal at an earlier time. So, having said that, let's begin with the chapter totally devoted to Leviathan, the Curse of the Levitical Priests; it, you might recall, is located in Chapter 41 of the Book of Job. We, however, will not be looking at all 34 verses but only a small handful. Let's start with verse three; it says:

"Will he make many supplications unto
Thee? will he speak soft words unto thee?

Well, I can definitely tell you this. Eli surely didn't speak
soft words to a sweet and godly woman named Hannah.
He was rude, mean, and what he did say to her was absolutely undeserved. Poor Hannah found out exactly what
it's like when you have to deal with the future antichrist.
Here, you see for yourself:

"Then said Elkanah her husband to her,
Hannah, why weepests thou? and why
Eatest thou not? and why is thy heart
Grieved? am not I better to thee than
Ten sons? So Hannah rose up after they
Had eaten in Shiloh, and after they had
Drunk. Now Eli the priest sat upon a
Seat by a post of the temple of the Lord,
And she was in bitterness of soul, and
Prayed unto the Lord, and wept sore.
And it came to pass, as she continued
Praying before the Lord, that Eli marked
Her mouth. Now Hannah, she spake in her
Heart; only her lips moved, but her voice
Was not heard: therefore Eli thought

> She had been drunken. And Eli said unto
> Her, How long wilt thou be drunken?
> Put away thy wine from thee."
> 1 Samuel 1: 8-10; 12-14

Wow, how cruel were Eli's words to poor, sweet Hannah? They were mean and vicious and something the lofty antichrist would unquestionably say. We are told exclusively that he was watching her pray, even "marking" her mouth. Now, I am aware of the fact that the writer of this passage tells us that Eli thought Hannah was drunk, but Eli was the High Priest in Shiloh. Surely and without question, he previously witnessed many people pray *exactly* like Hannah did with just the moving of her lips. Plus, is that really how a drunken person in those same, exact circumstances as Hannah would actually act? I'd have to say categorically, "No." A drunk is usually loud and deliberately causes *wanted* attention as well as an embarrassing scene, even if they really don't want it. Hannah was just the opposite; she was quiet and reverent, inconspicuous and to herself; and, more importantly, God's word actually says that she *wasn't* drunk but, rather, in great deep sorrow.

Alright, there's another word in that previous passage that I would now like to examine; it's the word, "marked," and it means, among other things, to "hedge about...guard..."[21] So, with the true definition of the word now being understood, it is quite clear that Eli wasn't just watching her lips move and, therefore, simply thought that she was drunk; no, that wasn't the case at all; he *knew* she was praying all along and was obviously threatened by it, so he, as the true meaning of the word actually indicates, internally put a hedge around her mouth, so to speak, because he didn't know what she was saying (Remember, "...her voice was not heard:"). The fact of the matter is, for all he knew, she was, indeed, aware of his blatant and disgusting hypocrisy (She most likely was very well aware of it. I do not believe for a second that her actually referring to Belial [1 Samuel 1: 16] – a known reference to a very evil presence -- while speaking to Eli at the very, same time just happens to be a mere coincidence; no, I don't believe that at all.), and she very well could've been praying about him; so, he "marked" her mouth in what was evidently a defensive and concerned move that was rooted in worry and guilt. Why do I say, "guilt?" Well, because he without question was a total failure as God's High Priest, and he even knew it himself; he also knew that he didn't belong to God, so, consequently, he experienced guilt and conviction, not just

---

[21] Ibid., 145

because of his dreadful and wicked actions as a high priest and as a human being, but also because he wholeheartedly knew that the Father was not his God. Also, because he felt threatened and became concerned while watching Hannah pray, he deliberately accused her of being drunk just so that – watch this – he could entice a response out of her and *really* find out what she was praying; he knew that by just accusing her of being drunk, she would go ahead and defend herself by telling him the truth (which she did) and tell him exactly what she was saying in her Specifically, he wanted to know if her prayer was about her praying for help from God regarding Eli and his evil behavior at the temple in Shiloh; that's what he was precisely concerned about; and that's why he accused her of being drunk, not because he actually *thought* she was drunk, but so that he could find out the exact contents of her prayer, and, therefore, in his mind, hopefully relieve the threatening and worrisome feelings that he was experiencing as well as the deep, overwhelming feelings of guilt, worry and fear that clearly filled his heart and mind and even caused him to say such cruel and undeserving words to Hannah in the first place.

Well, guess what? Hannah wasn't the only person who did not receive gentle and soft words from Eli. Nope, she sure wasn't. There was also another person, a young, sweet child by the name of Samuel who also found himself in a living nightmare, literally looking into the evil and scary eyes of Leviathan, and hearing for himself the hurtful and cruel words that surely caused every hair on his little body to stand and rise in overwhelming fear; but before you read about Samuel's personal nightmare, please, if you will, allow me to first set the scene: Samuel was just told by God that judgment is going to fall on Eli and his whole house. God said, "In that day I will perform against Eli all things which I have spoken concerning his house (1 Samuel 3: 12):" Well, Samuel was afraid to tell Eli (Gee, I wonder why.) what God told him; so, Eli, being the Curse of the Levitical Priests that he is, actually threatened and even deliberately intimidated that little boy (Yeah, can you believe that – threatening, intimidating a child! What a bully! What a loser!). What did Eli say? Eli told Samuel that if he didn't tell him what God said, God would pronounce the very judgment, the *very curse* that was spoken against Eli, to fall on sweet Samuel instead. Now, that's a lie! He deliberately lied to poor Samuel! Wow, can you believe that? What a loser Eli is! What a horrible human being and total failure Eli was as God's High Priest; and poor Samuel, imagine what he personally experienced having to deal with that cursed beast of a man, Eli, face to face, literally looking into his sinful eyes, hearing his scary, ugly voice, and feeling his eerie and evil presence. Wow, imagine that! Imagine experiencing what poor Samuel had to go through. He must've been literally scared to death! As for me, now, that's definitely not something that I ever want to experience!

Ok, the following passage is the actual personal encounter between Samuel and Eli:

> "Then Eli called Samuel, and said, Samuel,
> My son. And he answered, Here am I. And
> He [Eli] said, What is the thing that the Lord
> Hath said unto thee? I pray thee hide it not
> From me; God do so to thee, and more also,
> If thou hide any thing from me of all the things
> That he said unto thee."
> 1 Samuel 3: 16-17

The words Eli spoke to Samuel definitely weren't soft, but what is worse is how Eli used God as a means, a forceful means to threaten, intimidate, and ultimately scare little Samuel into doing exactly what he wanted. Now, if that isn't child abuse, then I'm not sure how it is correctly defined.

Oh, boy, the following passage is what some people would refer to as a "whopper" or, perhaps, this just might be your own personal "Aha!" moment where the light of understanding goes on (That is if it hasn't already.), and you finally realize that Eli really *is* the antichrist. Nevertheless, it is *so extremely* insightful and *so incredibly* significant; it directly -- I mean, directly – points exclusively at Eli; it really does. How? Well, it does so by literally speaking of his death; that's right, his death is most assuredly spoken in that verse. You see, as we discovered earlier with the help from one of the five, major clues, Eli irrefutably died from a medical stroke – that was his "deadly wound" spoken of in Revelation 13 – but, as a result from his catastrophic stroke, he also suffered – get this – a broken neck. Yep, that's right! He really did! Eli's neck was broken! Boy, this historic and personal fact regarding Eli is such an important clue that holds *so* much amazing revelations that I can barely type right now – seriously; but anyway, that's how this extremely significant and, yes, even symbolic (as you will no doubt find out a little later … if you keep reading) clue located in this teensy-weensy, little verse speaks of and points directly at Eli. So, would you now like the proof? Ok, here it is:

"And there ran a man of Benjamin out of

The army, and came to Shiloh the same
Day with his cloths rent, and with earth
Upon his head. And when he came, lo,
Eli sat upon a seat by the wayside watching;
For his heart trembled for the ark of God,
And when Eli heard the noise of the crying,
He said, What meaneth the noise of this
Tumult? And the man came in hastily,
And told Eli. Now Eli was ninety and
Eight years old; and his eyes were dim,
that he could not see. And the man said
Unto Eli, I am he that came out of the
Army, and I fled today out of the army,
And he [Eli] said, What is there done,
My son? And the messenger answered
And said, Israel is fled before the Philistines,
And there hath been also a great slaughter
Among the people, and thy two sons also,
Hophni and Phineas, are dead, and the ark
Of God is taken. And it came to pass, when
He made mention of the ark of God, that he
Fell from off the seat backward by the side
Of the gate, and his neck brake, and he died:
For he was an old man and heavy. And he

Had judged Israel forty years."
1 Samuel 4: 12-18

Alright, what I'd like to do now is turn your attention to
a very important passage of scripture. Here it is:

> "In the beginning of the reign of Jehoiakim
> The son of Josiah king of Judah came this
> Word from the Lord, saying, Thus saith the
> Lord; Stand in the court of the Lord's house,
> All the words that I command thee to speak
> Unto them; diminish not a word: If so be
> They will hearken, and turn every man from
> His evil way, that I may repent me of the evil,
> Which I purpose to do unto them because
> Of the evil of their doings. And thou shalt
> Say unto them, Thus saith the Lord; if ye
> Will not hearken to me, to walk in my law,
> Which I have set before you, To hearken to
> The words of my servants the prophets,
> Whom I sent unto you, both rising up early,
> And sending them, but ye have not hearkened;
> Then will I make this house like Shiloh, and
> Will make this city a curse to all the nations

Of the earth."
Jeremiah 26: 1-6

This verse has to be one of the most impactful, significant verses relating to Eli; it really is. As I have said before, all of the scriptures are priceless and their worth is immeasurable, but wow, did you happen to catch what God said in that last sentence? Wow! I mean, *Wow!* God actually made mention of Eli's former place of residence, the city of Shiloh, and in the very, same sentence, He literally mentioned a curse, which is obviously an insinuation and a clue and even a direct acknowledgement that not only did a curse really exist in the city of Shiloh, but more importantly, the curse was in the form of a man, that man has a name, and his name is, in fact, none other than Eli. Wow, can you believe *that?* Now, that is totally riveting as well as down-right amazing! Unquestionably, God is actually giving us several clues just by this one sentence, and by *His very own words* and, more importantly, *His* acknowledgment of a curse that actually existed not just in the city of Shiloh but also in the temple itself, a number of things can now both biblically and factually be concluded; these conclusions, by the way, prove even the more that what has already been stated in this book, is not only totally accurate but is also 100% the truth. Here, now, are those God-given, Spirit-filled conclusions that can be understandably made based on what God said regarding Eli, the city of Shiloh, and an actual curse:

1. In the city of Shiloh, there was a curse.
2. The city of Shiloh was a curse to other cities.
3. In the Lord's temple located in Shiloh, there was a curse.
4. That curse in the Lord's temple located in Shiloh was Eli.
5. Eli while in Shiloh was a curse to the people.
6. Eli is the Curse of the Levitical Priests.
7. Eli is Leviathan.
8. Eli is the antichrist.
9. Eli, as both Leviathan and the antichrist, will be "a curse to all the nations of the earth."

One word: Wow.

Thus far, *all* of those above conclusions have been biblically and factually proven, but I feel number two, "The city of Shiloh was a curse to other cities" and number five, "Eli while in Shiloh was a curse to the people" could use just a little bit more scriptural proof. Therefore, the following

passage proves even the more that disgusting sin and even
a curse was alive and well in the city of Shiloh:

> "Now the sons of Eli were sons of Belial; they
> Knew not the Lord. And the priests' custom
> With the people was, that, when any man
> Offered sacrifice, the priest's servant came,
> While the flesh was in seething, with a fleshhook
> Of three teeth in his hand; and he struck it into
> The pan, or kettle, or caldron, or pot; all that
> The fleshhook brought up the priest took for
> Himself [This was irreverent worship; Leviticus
> 3: 1-5]. So they did in Shiloh unto all the
> Israelites that came thither. Also before they
> Burnt the fat, the priest's servant came and
> Said to the man that sacrificed, Give flesh to
> Roast for the priest; for he will not have sodden
> Flesh of thee, but raw. And if any man said
> Unto him, Let them not fail to burn the fat
> Presently, and then take as much as thy soul
> Desireth; then he would answer him, Nay;
> But thou shalt give it me now: and if now, I
> Will take it by force. Wherefore the sin of
> The young men was very great before the
> LORD: for men abhorred the offering of the

Lord [People hated to worship there because
Of All the sin, irreverent worship, and the fact
That there was a curse in human form presiding
over the entire worship process there in Shiloh.]."
1 Samuel 2: 12-17

"For they provoked him to anger with their high
Places, and moved him to jealousy with their
Graven images. When God heard this, he was
Wroth, and greatly abhorred Israel: So that he
.Forsook the tabernacle of Shiloh, the tent which
.he placed among men;"
Psalm 78; 58-60

Ok, we're now moving on to our next topic to be examined; it was first mentioned in the second, major clue,
"His Deadly Wound," and it revolves around this verse
right here:

> "...the beast [Eli], which had the wound by a
> Sword, and did live."
> Revelation 13: 14

Alright, the word that we want to focus in on is the word,
"sword," and it literally means in a figurative sense "judicial

punishment."[22] So, what God's word is telling us is that Eli's death was not only warranted and well-deserving but, more importantly, it was personally given and exclusively handed down by God Himself; yep, that's right. God *alone* executed judgment on Eli, and his death is totally and only as a result of him *forsaking* God; *that's* what God's word is saying, and that's why Eli was slain with the sword of a stroke. I should also point out that the word "judicial" means that Eli's death was pronounced and spoken by a judge. Well, I now have a question for you: Is God a judge too? Yes, He sure is, and here's the proof:

> "The Lord shall judge the people:"
> Psalms 7: 8

Alright, we're moving right along. Let's go ahead and take a look at the next topic that will now demand our attention; it revolves around the same clue, "His Deadly Wound," and is based off of this verse right here:

> "Woe to the idol shepherd [Eli, the antichrist] that leaveth the flock! the Sword shall be upon his arm, and upon His right eye: his arm shall be

---

[22] Ibid., 55

clean Dried up, and his right eye shall be Utterly darkened."
Zechariah 11: 17

Now, for those of you who have always stayed true to the scripturally based belief that one day the antichrist's arm and right eye will somehow, some way experience a very unhealthy, abnormal condition, then kudos to you, because although you are not entirely right, you are, however, *very* close to the truth. You see, the meaning of the above verse speaks of the stroke that actually killed Eli *the first time;* yep, that's right; this verse, in fact, speaks directly of his "deadly wound." Therefore, this verse is not just a mere clue; it is not just simply more irrefutable proof of Eli really being the antichrist. No, this verse literally speaks in graphic detail the actual symptoms of the stroke that God righteously inflicted upon Eli. Wow, can you believe *that?* Now, that is totally amazing!

There's also another point regarding this verse, and it is this: God is sending Eli a very personal message; yes, He certainly is, and what God is saying is that just like He already disposed of Eli through the means of a catastrophic stroke, He will, in fact, do it again. In effect, God is very clearly reminding Eli – even warning him – that he shouldn't forget what God previously did to him, and that God will most definitely do it once again after Eli is satanically resurrected and returns back to Planet Earth as the antichrist. Wow! Now, that is just awesome!

Alright, to be sure, strokes are bad -- very bad. The symptoms that go along with strokes vary and are all potentially devastating. Here are just some of the symptoms:

- Arm weakening
- loss of balance or coordination
- Vision issues or sight out of one eye
- Wooziness

Now, what I'd like to say is this: Before God revealed to me that Eli is the antichrist, I always thought it was a little strange that Eli fell off of his seat backwards in the first place; I really did. In fact, it made no sense to me, and I never really understood it. At that time, I just thought it was some freak accident or crazy circumstance that caused him to fall backwards off of his seat. "Maybe it was the way he was sitting," I thought. "Maybe he was just leaning too much to one side," I earnestly thought, as I tried to fully understand the actual reason; but, as usual, it wasn't until God so graciously revealed to me the correct answer that I finally an fully understood. Having said that, allow me to now ask a question of you: Why do you think Eli fell off of his chair, backwards (The correct answer, by the way, is located in what you just read.)? Well, the answer is that it was the symptoms of the stroke that suddenly came upon Eli that literally seized his brain and caused him to experience all sorts of awful sensations and devastating symptoms such as wooziness, loss of balance or coordination, and arm weakening; *that's* what caused Eli to lose his balance and fall; *that's* what caused him to fall backwards; obviously, it was those catastrophic and destructive stroke symptoms that made him fall backwards off of his chair, and thanks to God, I might add, we now know the truth.

Alright, up next we're going to take a look at a very special prayer spoken by a very special lady, a lady that actually reminds me of my ma. You might remember this lady's name (I mentioned her earlier.). Her name is Hannah. She's the mother of Samuel, and this is her amazing prayer:

> "...My heart rejoiceth in the Lord, mine horn
> Is exalted in the Lord: my mouth is enlarged
> Over mine enemies; because I rejoiceth in thy
> Salvation. There is none holy as the Lord: for
> There is none beside thee: neither is there any

Rock like our God. Talk no more so exceeding
Proudly; let not arrogancy come out of your
Mouth: for the Lord is a God of knowledge,
And by him actions are weighed. The bows of
The mighty men are broken, and they that
Stumbled are girded with strength. They that
Were full have hired out themselves for bread;
And they that were hungry ceased: so that
The barren hath born seven; and she that has
Many children has waxed feeble. The Lord
Killeth, and maketh alive: he bringeth down
To the grave, and bringeth up. He raiseth up
The poor out of the dust, and lifteth up the
Beggar from the dunghill, to set them
Among princes, and to make them inherit
The throne of glory: for the pillars of the
Earth are the Lord's, and he hath set the
World upon them. He will keep the feet
Of the saints, and the wicked shall be silent
In darkness; for by strength shall no man
Prevail. The adversaries of the Lord shall
Be broken to pieces; out of heaven shall he
Thunder upon them: the Lord shall judge
The ends of the earth; and he shall give
Strength unto his king, and exalt the horn

Of his anointed."
1 Samuel 2: 1-10

So, did you happen to notice the times when Eli was personally addressed? Certainly, he was, and because God did not reveal everything to me concerning Eli, there are, unfortunately, instances in Hannah's prayer and possibly elsewhere that I just don't see. On the positive side, what God has revealed to me, I will also, in turn, reveal to you.

Let's begin examining the part in Hannah's prayer where she says, "my mouth is enlarged over mine enemies." Now, how interesting is *that?* Earlier, we are told in God's word that Eli "marked" her mouth, and we now know exactly what that word means as well as why he marked her mouth in the first place; and what does Hannah actually say here in her prayer? Wow! She actually says that her mouth is *enlarged* over her enemies, meaning that, if I may paraphrase, "Listen, Eli, you and me are not the same. I serve the Lord, and you serve the devil; we are enemies. I don't care if you don't want me to pray to my Father. It's not my fault that you feel threatened and scared. My mouth will *always* speak to my Father, and if that includes prophesying about you and your demise, then that is what my mouth will speak."

Alright, the next verse we'll now look at is this one: "Talk no more so exceeding proudly; let not arrogancy come out of your mouth." Ok, I'll give you one guess – just one -- as to who this statement is solely directed to and speaks of 100%. *Obviously,* the one person that Hannah is referring to is none other than Eli, and this verse speaks of and thoroughly proves Eli to be well named -- "lofty." Evidently, while in Eli's twisted and evil presence, Hannah witnessed first hand just how filled with pride Eli really is, and no doubt she must've been very displeased, to say the least. Lastly, I'm willing to bet that I'm definitely not the only one who knows Eli to be the biggest loser in the world.

Here, now, is the next verse that we will look at:

> "The Lord killeth, and maketh alive: he Bringeth
> down to the grave, and bringeth up."
> Verse 6

Basically, this verse prophetically speaks of Eli's future as Hannah had foresaw it; yes, it really does. How? Well, after Hannah's mouth was enlarged by God over her diabolical enemy, Eli, and, therefore, spoke these very words, Eli had judgment pronounced on him by God [1 Samuel

3: 11-14] and, as a result, was served with Godly punishment [1 Samuel 4: 18] which is, in fact, the "deadly wound" of Revelation Chapter 13; this punishment came in the form of a stroke, and Eli was brought down to the grave. However, just as Hannah prophesied here in this verse, Eli will one day be allowed by God to experience a resurrection from the Bottomless Pit of Hell where he currently is right now and will be brought back up to Planet Earth where he will ultimately become the Curse of the Levitical Priests, Leviathan, the antichrist.

This verse also makes it very clear that it is absolutely not by Eli's strength or even by Satan's, for that matter, that will cause Eli to actually leave the Bottomless Pit of Hell. This verse makes it 100% clear to Eli, Satan, and literally everyone else who reads God's word that it is *only* because of God and by His incredible, supernatural power and authority and perfect will that Eli will one day be allowed to leave the pit and experience an indescribable astounding resurrection.

Ok, we're doing good. Here's the next verse we will now observe:

"...the wicked shall be silent in darkness;

For by strength shall no man prevail."
Verse 9

Clearly and once again, this is a direct reference to Eli. Notice please that Hannah says that no *man* will prevail by strength, meaning that no matter how strong Eli is when he is amazingly resurrected out of Hell, he is *still* a man; and more specifically, Eli was a man before being struck down with a stroke, he died as a man, and he will one day return as a man, albeit the most wicked man ever who will be thoroughly empowered by the most powerful, most wicked angel that exists, but nonetheless, he's still a man.

As you read earlier, Eli, when he returns back to earth as the antichrist, will eventually be defeated by God in battle and will be thrown into a very dark and horrible place known as Hell; some kings will also be there. Well, when these kings see him return for a *second* time, they will be shocked to see him and will say:

> "…Is this the man that made the earth
> To tremble, that did shake kingdoms;
> That made the world as a wilderness,
> And destroyed the cities thereof; that

Opened not the house of the prisoners?
...thou art cast of thy grave like an abominable
Branch, and as the raiment of those that are
Slain, thrust through with a sword, that go
Down to the stones of the pit; as a carcase
Trodden under feet. Thou shalt not be
Joined with them in burial, because thou
Hast destroyed thy land, and slain thy
People: the seed of the evildoers shall
Never be renowned."
Isaiah 14: 16-17; 19-20

Alright, with that we are now finished looking at Hannah's marvelous prayer. We will now take a look at a very popular verse that has seriously caused quite a stir as well as received a lot of attention and countless number of theories as to its true, correct meaning. It's fair to say that for thousands of years this verse has prevailed over those countless number of theories and has escaped being correctly understood until now. So, without further ado, here it is:

"Neither shall he [Eli] regard the...desire
Of women."
Daniel 11: 37

Believe it or not, this verse does, in fact, speak of Eli in a sexual sense. More importantly, it gives further proof and even further credence to the unquestionable fact that when he is resurrected out of the Bottomless Pit of Hell, his body will, indeed, be a spiritual body, one that will be made up of spiritual flesh and spiritual bone. How does it give further proof? Oh, that's easy. Well, first of all, this verse evidently tells us that Eli will not have the normal, sexual interest towards women. Now, at this time, you should ask yourself this one question: Why is that? Why is it that Eli will not have any interest or, shall I say, not have any "…desire of…" -- or for (Either conjunction is fine; that is precisely the implication the Prophet Daniel was making when he wrote down this verse.) -- women in a sexual way? Well, that's because as a spirit, Eli will have absolutely *no blood* inside of his body; yep, that's right. No blood will circulate in his body. Why? Well, that's because he will not *need* blood to be alive and remain alive. You see, humans that have not yet died such as you and I absolutely must have blood to live and remain living, but a spirit has no need for blood. Even Gods word speaks of this truth, saying that the very life of human flesh that has not yet tasted death is found in the blood. Here, you see for yourself:

> "For it [blood] is the life of all flesh; the Blood of
> it is for the life thereof...for the Life of all flesh is
> the blood thereof:"
> Leviticus 17: 14

Right about now you're probably thinking and asking in your head (or perhaps out loud), "What does blood have to do with Eli not having the desire of women in a sexual way?" Well, I must say, that's a very good question, but here's the answer: That's where hormones come in; yep, that's right. I said, "hormones." You see, testosterone is one of the main hormones in a man's body, and it is also one of the primary causes for a man having – u guess it – a desire for women in a sexual way. So, have said all that, the reason why Eli will not "...regard the...desire of women" when he comes back to earth after being resurrected from the pit is because of the following reasons:

1. He will not have a physical body like he once had in the .past.
2. Because his body will not be a physical body, he,. therefore, will not possess blood.
3. Because he will not possess blood, he will, there- fore, *also* not possess blood derived hormones and, specifically, testosterone which, as stated earlier, is

factually known to produce a natural, God-given, *sexual* desire for women.

4. His body will be a spiritual body, one, in fact, made up of spiritual flesh and spiritual bone with literally no blood, no hormones, and absolutely no testosterone.

Well, there you have it. Now you know why Eli will not "...regard the...desire of women." It is no doubt very interesting, to say the least.

Lastly, it should be stated that Eli's resurrected body will be similar to that of The Lord Jesus' body. Incredibly, he will be able to eat and consume food (Luke 24: 41-43), transcend the physical world like, for example, by being able to walk through closed doors (John 20: 19), possess the amazing ability to literally elevate his body and even fly (Luke 24: 50-51), and, understandably, cause people to be thoroughly terrified when they see him with their very own eyes (Luke 24: 37;41).

Alright, one last point to make and then this chapter will be complete. Here goes: It should be noted that when Eli was on earth, apparently, he was heterosexual. While there is no mention of him actually having a wife or being married, the scriptures do state (as we witnessed earlier) that he was, indeed, a father and a father of those two loser sons of his, Hophni and Phineas.

Well, that's it for this chapter. Hopefully, you enjoyed it and also found all those irrefutable truths that were presented earlier to not be too difficult to grasp. Personally, I feel that out of all the chapters thus far in this book, this one, without a doubt, is filled with the most shocking, most astonishing, and most incredibly eye-opening, God-given and prophetic truths that one could have ever been given. Well, having said that, one things for sure: More startling, more eye-opening, God-given and Spirit-filled truths are on the way, truths that will, once again, cause your socks to be blown right off your feet, truths that will make your hair stand straight up no matter how curly it may be, and truths that will open your mouth so wide that all you'll be able to see is the outside of your upper lip! Yes, I'm serious! I kid you not! You'll be totally amazed at the shocking truths that are in store for you! So, hold on tight to that chair of yours, quickly put your socks back on, and hurry up and fix your upper lip, because this exhilarating, thrilling, and truly unforgettable ride isn't over just yet!

God Loves You and Symbolism Too

I KNOW. SOMETIMES IT'S HARD TO BELIEVE that God really does love you. You look at all the horrible things going on in the world, and they make you feel so depressed, so confused, and so hopeless; and then, you understandably, begin to question God's perfect love not just for yourself but for others as well. I understand. I really do, but what we need to continually remind ourselves is that while God made everything and solely by His unmatched and unfathomable power put everything into existence, there is, however, a *very* evil, extremely dark, and powerful presence in this world today, a presence so corrupt that it goes against literally everything that God intended the world to be from the very beginning, a presence that is completely the direct opposite of God and what He represents, and a presence *who* was the actual originator of wickedness, pain, and sin, the one who is *really* responsible for evil coming into existence in the first place as well as why this planet that we live on is so filled with awful, depressing, and Holy Spirit-grieving events; this selfish, prideful, disgusting presence belongs to Satan and his wicked, angelic host; *they* are the ones solely responsible for *everything* you see that's bad and wrong happening in the world – everything, from sickness and disease to abuse and even murder, everything that you, unfortunately, witness and watch happening with your very own eyes in your very own life as well as the lives of others, is the direct result of the wretched, despicable, and sinful, me-first attitude of the evil one, Satan. *He's* the one who is totally responsible for all of the hurt, all of the pain, all of the suffering, all of the wrong, all of the unfairness, all of the injustice – everything; it's *him* who is the one to blame, and him who is entirely at fault, not God. Let this truth be understood and understood to the fullest: God *is* love; His love is perfect and everlasting, and He absolutely – without question – loves you.

To be sure, the following scriptures prove that it is Satan who is not only at work in this world, but it is him who is solely responsible for all of the evil that you and I see in our lives and in the lives of others:

"Be sober, be vigilant; because your adversary
The devil, as a roaring lion, walketh about, Seeking
whom he may devour."
1 Peter 5: 8

"...ye walked according to the course of this World,
according to the prince of the power Of the air
[Satan], the spirit that now worketh In the children of disobedience."
Ephesians 2: 2

See, it really is entirely Satan's fault that this world is so
messed up. Satan is the evil one, not God. Satan is the
one who wants to hurt you and make you cry, not God.
Satan is the one who lies to you and purposely tries to
deceive you, not God. Satan is the one who wants to literally destroy you and totally ruin your life, not God. Satan,
the original creator of evil and sin, is the one who wants
you dead, not God. Oh, no, God is love, and He loves you
very, very, much; here, now, is the proof:

"...for God is love."
1 John 4: 8

"We love him, because he first loved us."
1 John 4: 19

Alright, take a guess, if you will, as to what God also loves. Go ahead – guess. If you guessed symbolism, you are 100% correct. Boy, let me tell you: God absolutely is enthralled with and, unquestionably, has a huge hankering for symbolism. Yep, He sure does, and if you don't believe me, then get a load of this:

> "Then Jacob continued on his journey and
> Came to the land of the eastern peoples.
> There he saw a well in the field, with three
> Flocks of sheep lying near it because the
> Flocks were watered from the well. The
> Stone over the mouth of the well was large.
> When all the flocks were gathered there, the
> Shepherds would roll the stone away from the
> Well's mouth and water the sheep. Then they
> Would return the stone to its place over the
> Mouth of the well. Jacob asked the shepherds,
> "My brothers, where are you from?" "We're
> From Haran," they replied. He said to them,
> "Do you know Laban, Nahor's grandson?"
> "Yes, we know him," they answered. Then

Jacob asked them, "Is he well?" "Yes, he is,"
They said, "and here comes his daughter
Rachel with the sheep." "Look," he said, "the
sun is still high; it is not time for the flocks to
be gathered. Water the sheep and take them
back to pasture." "We can't," they replied,
"until all the flocks are gathered and the stone
Has been rolled away from the mouth of the
Well. Then we will water the sheep."
Genesis 29: 1-8

So, did you happen to see all of the symbolism that is stuffed within that passage? Did ya? It certainly is there, and there is also a symbolic theme nesting throughout the passage itself. Well, the first part of this truly amazing, symbolic passage that we are specifically going to look at is the part where it says, "There he saw a well in the field..." The field symbolically represents the world, as explained by the Lord Jesus Himself after speaking a parable to a great multitude of people that included – you guessed it – a field. Here, take a look:

"The field is the world;"
Matthew 13: 38

Next up: "...with three flocks of sheep..." I think it would be totally understandable if I were to say that sheep *always* symbolically represent people who really do belong to God – Christian people – who have humbly repented of their sins, have literally became His children by personally accepting His Son, the Lord Jesus Christ, and who will one day be given the exclusive right to eat from the most beautiful and truly indescribable tree, the Tree of Life, which wonderfully flourishes in Heaven (Revelation 22: 2). Here, you see for yourself:

> "My [the Lord Jesus] sheep hear my voice, And I
> know them, and they follow me:"
> John 10: 27

> "I [the Lord Jesus] am the good shepherd, And
> know my sheep, and am known of mine."
> John 10: 14

Alright, it should be pointed out that the word "three" in the symbolic verse, "...with three flocks of sheep..." is one of God's favorite numbers, and it actually references Him; this is true. I tell you no lie. The following list is proof of this fact, and in honor of God, three examples – well, I had to keep up with the theme, didn't I? -- will be given. Here they are:

- God consists of *three* individuals: The Holy Father, The Holy Son, and The . Holy Ghost (Matthew 28: 18-19).
- The Lord Jesus lived to be *33* years old (Luke 3: 23; 13: 6-7).
- On day *three,* the Lord Jesus rose from the dead (Matthew 20: 17-19).

See, I told you so. The number three in the verse "...with three flocks of sheep..." makes it very clear as well as symbolizes the fact that these three flocks of sheep absolutely belong to none other than God.

Now, we will look at just two words within that symbolic passage of Genesis 29, and they are, "...the shepherds..." The shepherds represent the Angels of God, and just like the shepherds in Genesis 29 visited Jacob, God's real life angels also actively visit with people here on Planet Earth. Here's the proof:

> "Be not forgetful to entertain strangers:
> For thereby some have entertained angels
> Unawares."
> Hebrews 13: 2

"Are they [God's angels] not all ministering Spirits, sent for to minister for them who Shall be heirs of salvation?"
Hebrews 1: 14

"Take heed that ye despise not one of these Little ones; for I [the Lord Jesus] say unto you, That in Heaven their angels do always Behold the face of my Father which is in Heaven."
Matthew 18: 10

Ok, the next part of Genesis 29 – that awesome symbolic passage – that we will look at now also has just two words and they are as follows: "...the sun..." The word, "sun" represents none other than the Son of God, the Lord Jesus Christ. Oh, would you like to see the proof of this clear-cut fact? Ok, here it is:

"For the Lord God is a sun..."
Psalms 84: 11

"...and his [the Lord Jesus] countenance Was as the sun shineth in his strength."
Revelation 1: 16

So, the good news is that based on those two scriptural references, every time you wake up in the morning and see the light of day, know that it is symbolically representative of the brilliant, pure, and holy light that gracefully and lovingly radiates out from the Son of God, the Lord Jesus Christ.

Moving on, here's our next part that we will now examine: "...the sun is still high; it is not time for the flocks to be gathered." Notice, if you will, that the sun is still *high*. The word "high" is symbolic for Heaven (Well, it is very high [Isaiah 66: 1] from us.). Therefore, this part of the verse means that the Lord Jesus is stillin – you guessed it – Heaven; that is the reason why the shepherd go on to say that it's not time for the sheep (who symbolically represent Christians) to be gathered, because, in essence, the Lord Jesus, the *Sun* of Righteousness has not returned for them.

In the following verse, we can see a perfect example of the angels actually doing just that – "gathering" a person by the name of Lazarus and personally escorting him into paradise – how nice:

> "And it came to pass, that the beggar Died, and
> was carried by the angels..."
> Luke 16: 22

Alright, the next verse that we will now look at is this one right here: "We can't," they replied, "until all the flocks are gathered and the stone has been rolled away from the mouth of the well. Then we will water the sheep." The stone is symbolic of the Holy Ghost; yep, it sure is. You see, the shepherds said that they cannot water the sheep *until* the stone has been removed. Therefore, the stone unquestionably symbolizes the Holy Ghost, because it is literally the Holy Ghost who is right now this very second restraining Satan from thinking it is his turn for Show and Tell Day on Planet Earth and deceitfully bursting onto the scene -- on God's green grass no less – and proudly showing off his new, shiny, and lofty toy – Eli The Antichrist. We can see the very proof of this unmistakable fact in the Apostle Paul's letter to the church in Thessalonica. Here, see for yourself:

> "For the mystery of iniquity doth already
> Work: only he who now letteth will let,
> Until he be taken out of the way."
> 2 Thessalonians 2: 7

Yeah, I know, that verse is a little hard to understand. Thank God we have Dr. Willmington to help us understand just exactly what this verse really means; he explains:

"Here Paul states that although the influence
Of the antichrist could be felt, even at that time,
His full power and program were being held in
Check by a restrainer. (Note – the words "letteth"
And "let" should be translated "hinder.")
Who or what is this powerful restrainer? There are
Several theories.
a. It is human government. However, this is
Unlikely, for Satan already exercises strong
Influence upon the kingdoms of mankind.
(See Mt. 4: 8)
b. It is angels. This too is remote. (See Jude 1: 9)
c. It is the Holy Spirit. This is by far the most
Logical conclusion. Dr. Charles Ryrie writes:
The pretribulation argument is simply this.
The restrainer is God..."[23]

---

[23] Dr. H.L. Willmington, *"Willmington's Guide to the Bible"* (Wheaton: Tyndale House Publishers Inc, 1984), 412

Ok, so with Dr. Willmington's very helpful explaining, it can be easily understood that the stone in Genesis 29 really does symbolically represent the Holy Ghost.

Well, check this out: Believe it or not, God, the Father is also personally symbolized within the Chapter of Genesis 29; yes, He sure is. Care to take a guess as to who it might be? Go ahead. No, it's not Jacob. Try again. Ok, I'll tell you: It's Laban. That's right, Laban. He's the one who personally symbolizes God, and he does it, actually, in a few ways. The first way that Laban symbolizes God is when Jacob asks the shepherds (Remember, the shepherds are symbolic of God's angels.), "Do you know Laban...?" Well, *of course* they know Laban. Of course, they do! He's their Master, their Creator, and even their Boss. *Of course,* they know Him; and that is why their answer is, "Yes, we know him." The next way that Laban symbolizes God is by Jacob, once again, asking the shepherds (angels), "Is he well?" Well, *of course* He's well! He's God! He's sovereignly and justly sitting on His heavenly throne right now! *Of course,* He's well! He's the Creator of the universe, the Maker of all things, the Eternal God! *Of course,* He's well; and that is why their answer is, "Yes, he is..." The last way that Laban symbolizes God is by the actual meaning of Laban's name. It means "white,"[24] and why is that so utterly significant? Well, simply because *every time* God in the scriptures, He is represented by the color of white; this is because white symbolizes righteousness with absolutely no presence of sin, and this is exactly what God is (among other holy and pure attributes) -- righteous. Simply put: If God were to come and live with us humans on earth, work a 9-5, go to the grocery store and to other places of interest like the rest of us do, the color of His car would *absolutely, unquestionably, and most definitely* be white (Likewise, because of His unmatched humility, the car that He would drive would probably be one of a humble variety like a Pinto or something similar like a Sprint, for example.). Anyway, the following verse is proof that the color of white really is symbolic of God:

"I [Daniel] beheld till the thrones were
Case down, and the Ancient of days did
Sit, whose garment was white as snow,
And the hair of his head like the pure

---

[24] Taken from *THE NEW STRONG'S EXHAUSTIVE CONCORDANCE OF THE BIBLE* by Strong, James, L.L.D., S.T.D., 68

wool."
Daniel 7: 9

Alright, our last point to look at in that awesome, symbolic passage is this verse right here: "...water the sheep." Notice please that the sheep (God's children) cannot be given the water until the stone (the Holy Ghost) is removed. So, what does the water here symbolize? Well, it actually symbolizes salvation both here and in Heaven. Yep, it sure does. It symbolizes salvation here on earth in terms of being able to live a new and much more meaningful, godly life aimed at pleasing God and serving others as opposed to the previous life once lived that was full of a selfish, me-first attitude without the peace that surpasses all understanding that is only found upon receiving salvation through the Lord Jesus Christ.

And the water also symbolizes the exclusive right of salvation that only Christian people receive upon entering a wonderful and truly unbelievable place called Heaven. Oh, you don't believe me? Ok, here's the proof for both of the symbolizations:

> "Jesus answered and said unto her, If thou
> Knewest the gift of God, and who it is that

Saith, to thee Give me to drink; thou
Wouldest have asked of him, and he would
Have given thee living water."
John 4: 10

"And he shewed me a pure river of water of life,
Clear as crystal, proceeding out of the throne
Of God and of the Lamb."
Revelation 22: 1

Ok, now that we looked at all of that amazing symbolism found within the Chapter of Genesis 29, a question now awaits: What is the symbolic theme? Well, come on, you can do it. Here, I'll ask again: What is the symbolic theme? Perhaps it would help if the key points were reviewed first; having said that, here they now are:

- The field is symbolic of the world.
- The sheep are symbolic of Christians.
- The shepherds are symbolic of God's angels.
- The sun is symbolic of the Lord Jesus.
- The stone is symbolic of the Holy Ghost.
- The water is symbolic of salvation being experienced both here on earth and in Heaven as well.

So, there they are; there are the key, symbolic points. What do you think is the symbolic theme for Genesis 29? The answer: The Rapture. Yep, that's right – the Rapture. It is the true meaning and the symbolic theme that is hidden and tucked away but definitely can be seen in Genesis 29. Nice, huh?

May I say something? I just want to make it perfectly clear that it really was God who so graciously and undeservingly showed me the symbolic nature found in Genesis 29. It's only because of *Him* and by His divine grace and favor that I was able to reveal that awesome, symbolic passage to you. Just like Daniel once admitted to King Nebuchadnezzar of Babylon, I and my ability are no better than anyone else's on the face of this very planet:

> "But as for me, this secret is not revealed
> To me for any wisdom that I have more
> Than any living..."
> Daniel 2: 30

Just like my favorite prophet in the entire Holy Bible, the Prophet Elijah, acknowledged to God, I, too, am no better than any of the saints living or otherwise:

"...I am no better than my fathers."
Just like the patriarch Joseph freely spoke the truth
to the Pharaoh of Egypt, giving all the credit and
glory to God for revealing to him the meaning of
Pharaoh's dream, the *only* reason why I am able
to point out the incredible symbolism in Genesis
29 is because of God and God alone:
"And Joseph answered Pharaoh, saying,
It is not in me: God shall give Pharaoh an
Answer of peace."
Genesis 41: 16

Lastly, just like the Apostle Paul also stated the truth, the
truth to the church in Corinth regarding himself, I, too,
am absolutely *nothing* without the Vine (John 15: 5) --
my Lord and Savior, Jesus Christ:

"...though I be nothing."
2 Corinthians 12: 11

Well, as you read throughout this chapter, God not only
loves you very much, He also loves symbolism. Please, if
you will, keep that in mind because in the next chapter,
you will get the exclusive privilege of seeing how God
symbolized not just Himself many times in the scriptures,

but how he actually symbolized Eli. Yes, that's right, believe it or not, He certainly *did* symbolize Himself and even that loser, Eli; and the good news is all that and more is coming up next.

One quick note: Since one of the goals of this book is to keep the reader in as much suspense as possible, and because it would be very easy for anyone to discover who the antichrist is just by looking at the title of the next chapter, I have decided, once again, to not include Eli's name. Ok? So, the word, "he," will be used in place of his name. My hope in doing this is that the riveting suspense, gripping thrill, and total shock of finally discovering just who the antichrist really is, will not be sacrificed or ruined; having said that, this chapter is now complete.

He is an Ass

First of all, those words in the above title are God's, not mine. That's right; those are *His* words; they belong to Him and not me. Oh, I can just hear someone saying right now, "What do you mean? What do you mean those are His words and not yours?" Well, I must say, the reason why someone could possibly be offended at the title of this chapter, experience the not-so-good feelings associated with the potential offense that could go hand-in-hand from the above title, and might even ask those two, particular questions, is because they (the possible offended person) simply are just unaware of what God actually called Eli and, more importantly, what He specifically called Eli through the vehicle of symbolism; but that's Ok. I, too, was *completely* unaware of the truly incredible and fascinating symbolism pertaining to the antichrist – Eli – in The Holy Bible until the very moment God so graciously revealed it to me.

Personally, I feel that out of all -- I mean, *all* – the amazing clues, all the jaw-dropping information, all the relevant sub-topics, all the juicy tidbits, and all the incredible, God-given and Holy Ghost inspired insight that God undeservedly revealed to me, this one, factual, historical, and biblical truth has hands down affected me the most; it really has. This amazing and incomparable truth, to me, has been absolutely riveting, totally gripping, and down-right life changing. What factual, historical and biblical truth that is *so amazing* and down-right unforgettable am I talking about? Oh, just this one, this one right here:

> "And it shall be when the Lord shall bring
> Thee into the land of the Canaanites, as he
> Sware unto thee and to thy fathers, and
> Shall give it thee, That thou shall set apart
> Unto the Lord all that openeth the matrix,
> And every firstling that cometh of a beast
> Which thou hast; the males shall be the
> Lord's. And every firstling of an ass thou
> Shalt redeem with a Lamb; and if thou wilt
> Not redeem it, then thou shalt break his
> Neck."
> Exodus 13: 11-13

Whoa! Did you see that? Did you see what happened to the ass if it wasn't redeemed? Whoa! His neck was broken! Yeah, his *neck!* Now, I must ask you this question: Doesn't that sound a *little* familiar, even a *little?* Well, if it doesn't, it certainly should. Why? Oh, simply because (in case you forgot) that's *exactly* -- I mean, *exactly* -- what happened to Eli. Eli's very own, personal neck was broken, and if you are having a difficult time remembering, here, now, is the actual proof:

> "And it came to pass, when he made
> Mention of the ark of God, that he
> [Eli] fell from off the seat backward
> By the side of the gate, and his neck
> Brake, and he died."
> 1 Samuel 4: 18

Whoa! You see, the fact of the matter is that Eli, receiving a broken neck is *much more* than just an unfortunate accident; yep, it *certainly* is. Eli received a broken neck for a *reason!* He sure did! Here, now, is the *whole* truth; here's what *really* happened: Eli's neck was personally broken by God because God knew (He's God. He knows everything.) that Eli was never going to be redeemed – never. God knew that Eli was never going to turn from his wicked ways and stop being the ungodly person that he is, never going to humble himself and be the man of God that God truly desired him to be, never, ever going to personally experience the wonderful, incredible, and undeserved grace of God, the beautiful and marvelous grace that is freely offered as an unmerited gift by the merciful Father, the beautiful and marvelous grace that could have caused Eli to happily serve and live the rest of his days for the real God instead of the evil wannabe (Satan), and the beautiful and marvelous grace that, ultimately, could have brought him into the magnificent and glorious home of God instead of the Bottomless Pit of Hell where he is literally on fire and burning right now; and, you know, this marvelous and undeserved grace could have also prevented him from not having to deliberately and violently receive a broken neck in the first place and, in the process, be forever typified and personally labeled as a good-for-nothing ass.

You see, God instructed the patriarch Moses to give the firstborn ass to Him by means of a sacrifice; if, however, Moses chose – watch this – to redeem or *save* the firstborn ass, he had to save the ass by exclusively sacrificing a lamb. However, if Moses chose *not* to save the firstborn ass, then God told Moses to break his neck. Wow! That's just *amazing!* Can you believe *that?* Do you see all the incredible awesome symbolism going on with all these instructions? Do you? Do you see how all this is *unquestionably and obviously* linked to Eli and, more importantly, do you see how all these instructions point directly to his death and the absolute reason for why he suffered a broken neck in the first place? Do you? Wow, that's just amazing! I definitely remember when God first revealed this incredible, shocking, jaw-dropping, symbolic reference of truth concerning Eli and his death to me. Yep, I sure do. I was literally stunned for at least a week! I really was. I'm not lying! See, I told you; I told you that God really does love you and symbolism too!

Alright, one of the very important, symbolic references located within the symbolism of the ass is the animal that is used to actually redeem the ass; it is the lamb, and the reason why the lamb is *so* important, *so* incredibly meaningful, is because of *Who* the lamb actually represents; that's right. The Lamb does, indeed, represent Someone, and that "Someone" is none other than the Savior of the world, the Lord Jesus Christ, the One who literally had nails painfully go through His wrists and feet, immobilizing Him to an old rugged cross, the One who lovingly embraced as well as totally paid in full the penalty of our sin that was due – our *own*, personal sin-debt – and the One who *willingly* gave up His life for you and I so that we could one day joyfully and purposely live exclusively with Him forever in His beautiful and glorious place of residence – Heaven. In the following verse, we see the Lord Jesus' true representation as the Lamb of God; here's the proof:

> "The next day John seeth Jesus coming
> Unto him, and saith, Behold, the Lamb of
> God, which taketh away the sin of the
> World."
> John 1: 29

So, as you can see, God through that symbolic passage of the ass, is telling us *exactly* why He broke Eli's neck. The amazing Father is saying to us that the reason why He personally broke Eli's neck, is because God knew that Eli was going straight to the Bottomless Pit of Hell after dying; He also knew that one day in the future, Eli would eventually become the antichrist, so, because He knew that Eli would one day become the antichrist, and, obviously, never, *ever* repent, never be personally redeemed by the redeeming Lamb of God, the Lord Jesus Christ, God, in effect, had no other choice but to *not* redeem Eli.

Now, since God knew He was not ever going to redeem Eli, He gave symbolic instructions to Moses on exactly what to do with the unredeemed ass (who literally represents Eli), and He, therefore, did to Eli exactly as He instructed Moses to do with the unredeemed ass, the ass which was not personally redeemed with a lamb. What did He do to Eli? *He broke his neck!* That' what He did! He broke his neck! Wow! Incredible! That is utterly amazing! Can you believe *that?* I'm telling you: That is just incredible! Wow, if that clearly doesn't permanently classify Eli as an ass, if that doesn't specifically say just how spiritually lost Eli was and is as an individual, if that doesn't prove just how evil and worthless Eli actually is, then I don't know what does. Look here, if you had any doubts – *any* – as to Eli actually being the antichrist, you shouldn't have them anymore; no, you really shouldn't. Please don't make any mistake about it: Eli *is* absolutely evil; he *is* full of wickedness, and he is absolutely good for nothing, not to mention, he's also – without question and with all factual, historical, biblical and even symbolic certainty – the antichrist; and that truly incredible, symbolic passage regarding the unredeemed ass coupled with the fact that Eli really did suffer a broken neck, *absolutely proves* it even the more, even to beyond the exclusion of *any* reasonable doubt.

So, to be sure, that is where the amazing symbolism regarding Eli appears and can be seen; it appears exclusively in the breaking of the ass's neck; that's where it appears, and is also where Eli can obviously and clearly be seen. As a result, God believe it or not, is literally calling Eli an "ass." He really is, and that is, as most people would likely agree, not a good thing. Why? Well, number one, who wants to be referred to as an ass? Who wants that? No, not me. Plus, who wants to be called an ass by *God?* Oh, no, not me, *definitely* not me. Surely and without question, Eli personally being called an ass by God certainly is not positive in nature nor a good thing. Still, there is another reason for why it's not at all a good thing for Eli to be personally called an ass by God; yep, there sure is, and it is what the actual definition of the word, "ass," means. Yeah, you know, it means a very dumb person or a fool; and, for the record, *anyone* who knowingly turns down a wonderful and glorious eternity in Heaven with God, who actually loves you more than anyone else on the face of this planet, and, instead willingly chooses an unfathomable, indescribable, and hellish eternity full of torture, pain, suffering, and torment *has* to be stupid, has to be foolish, and most definitely, has to be an ass.

Well, guess what? The symbolism of the unredeemed ass has a second meaning, and that meaning is this: It represents those who deliberately reject God's redeeming Lamb, the savior of the world, the Lord Jesus Christ. You see, the unfortunate truth is that apart from being redeemed by the Lord Jesus, mankind is lost. That is why God provided the sinless and pure Lamb of God for humanity, so that through the sacrifice of His Lamb, man and his sin from his inherent, sinful nature could be forgiven. Make no mistake about it: God loves you, and He also provided The Way (John 14: 6) for you to be personally reconciled and redeemed to Him; and without Him, we are doomed to an everlasting life of pain, torture, and a very horrible existence without God. The proof of this sobering truth, by the way, is typified within the same verse of the instructions God gave to Moses regarding the ass. God said this:

> "and all the firstborn of man among your
> Children shall you redeem."
> Exodus 13: 13

Well, believe it or not, God called Eli an ass another time. He sure did, and here, now, is the proof:

> "And the Lord said unto me [Zechariah],

Take unto thee yet the instruments of a
Foolish shepherd [Eli]."
Zechariah 11: 15

Alright, as you learned earlier, God instructed Moses to break the neck of an ass if he chose not to redeem it through a sacrificial lamb. Now, some people may wonder or even question why – of all parts – God chose the neck to be broken. Well, apparently, He sees the neck as one of the many different ways that willful disobedience, rebellion, and sin are displayed in the human body. The following passages of scripture prove this, and are the supporting references:

"but he [Zedekiah] stiffened his neck,
And hardened his heart from turning
Unto the Lord God of Israel."
2 Chronicles 36: 13

"But they [Israel] obeyed not, neither
Inclined their ear, but made their neck
Stiff, that they might not hear, nor
Receive instruction."
Jeremiah 17: 23

See, God really does see the neck as one of the many parts of the body that shows willful rebellion towards Him; that is one of the reasons why He ultimately broke Eli's, and why He when describing Leviathan, the Curse of the Levitical Priests, clearly stated that his obstinate will to sin, disobey, and rebel against Him still is present. Here, you take a look for yourself:

> "In his neck remaineth strength..."
> Job 41: 22

Wow, imagine that. Even after being judicially punished and killed with a catastrophic stroke by the righteous Judge, even after receiving a broken neck and being symbolically labeled and typified as an ass of obstinacy, rebellion, and sin, even after being in the Bottomless Pit of Hell and burning in torment for thousands of years, even after one day in the future when he will experience total humiliation and defeat by God in battle, and even after one day in the future when he will also be thrown back again into the pit, Eli's neck – after experiencing all that – will still proudly and defiantly display his willful disobedience towards God. Wow, what a loser, what an ass – unredeemed, of course.

Well, I must say: God symbolizing Eli and putting it in His word really shouldn't come as any surprise to you. Why? Well, simply because He symbolized Himself. He sure did, so why then would He not symbolize Eli, *especially* since Eli *is* the antichrist, and the fact that the antichrist is such an important, biblical, and prophetic character who is mentioned and discussed many times and in many ways throughout the scriptures? Oh, I see. You want the proof, do you? Ok, fair enough. In the following passages, the Lord Jesus is first symbolized and then literally proved as the Lamb of God:

> "And Abraham said, My son, God will provide
> Himself a lamb for a burnt offering:"
> Genesis 22: 8

> "The next day John seeth Jesus coming unto
> Him, and saith, Behold, the Lamb of God,
> Which taketh away the sin of the world."
> John 1:29

The final scriptural references symbolically represent and literally prove that the Lord Jesus really is the Bread of Life. Here they are now:

"Then said the Lord unto Moses, Behold, I
Will rain bread from heaven [the Lord Jesus]
For you: and the people shall go out and
Gather a certain rate every day, that I may prove
Them, whether they will walk in my law, or no.
And in the morning the dew lay round about
The host. And when the dew that lay was gone
Up, behold, upon the face of the wilderness
There lay a small round thing, as small as the
Hoar frost on the ground. And when the
Children of Israel saw it, they said one to
Another, It is manna: for they wist not what
It was. And Moses said unto them, This is the
Bread which the Lord hath given you to eat."
Exodus 16: 4; 13-16

"Verily, verily, I [the Lord Jesus] say unto you,
He that believeth on me hath everlasting life.
I am that bread of life. Your fathers did eat
Manna in the wilderness, and are dead. This
Is the bread which cometh down from heaven,
That a man may eat thereof, and not die. I am
the living bread which came down from
heaven:"
John 6: 47-50

See, I told you. I told you that since the Lord Jesus symbolized Himself, it really should not come as any surprise at all that He would also personally symbolize Eli; and by Him doing so, it just further proves and totally cements the irrefutable fact that the unredeemed ass symbolically seen in the scriptures really is Eli.

Well, having said that, this chapter has now come to an end; but I do have just one more thing to say, and it is this: The gratefulness that I personally have within me is truly indescribable. I cannot speak the words necessary to describe just how thankful I am for my heavenly Father actually revealing all of these awesome truths to me. Seriously, who am I? I am absolutely nobody, and I am also nobody in the eyes of the world; but this I do know, and I know for a fact: While I am nobody without God, I am somebody with Him. The apostle Paul put it best when he said:

> "But by the grace of God I am what I
> Am."
> 1 Corinthians 15: 10

Oh Yes He Did

SO FAR, YOU HAVE BEEN GIVEN A LOT OF ASTON-
ishing, biblical, and factual truths, truths that literally
revealed to you the true nature and exact meaning of Eli's
deadly wound, truths that precisely identified Eli's actual
route that he will one day take as the antichrist, even
going so far as to reveal the literal name of the city that
Eli will eventually stay and remain in – the City of Nob,
the city of the priests – and lastly, truths that not only
revealed to you the irrefutable identity of the antichrist
but also his present, horrifying location, the Bottomless
Pit of Hell.

Well, I now have a question for you: What would u say
if I told you that the Redeemer, the Lamb of God, the
Lord Jesus *Himself,* not only spoke directly to Eli, but He
also positively and unquestionably identified him as the
antichrist? What would you say? Well, I tell you what:

You better start thinking of some words to say, because that's *exactly* what the Lord Jesus did. Oh, yes He did! He *absolutely* did! He literally said Eli's name! Here, now, is the astonishing, profound, and absolutely amazing proof:

> "And about the ninth hour Jesus cried
> With a loud voice, saying, ELI, ELI, LAMA
> SABACHTHANI?"
> Matthew 27: 46

Whoa! Did you see that? The Lord Jesus really *did* speak directly to Eli, and He also really did personally address him as the antichrist! *He really did!* The proof is right there before your very eyes! It really is! It's right there in that verse, right above this very word that you're reading right now! See, the Lord Jesus really *did* speak directly to Eli, and he really did identify him as the antichrist; and that's just amazing, I tell you, just utterly amazing!

Man, every time I think of this incredibly awesome fact, I just get excited. Why? Well, it's just that by the Lord Jesus directly calling out to Eli with a loud voice, He publicly and specifically identified Eli as the antichrist; oh, yes He did. He certainly did! No, don't make no mistake about it: He *exclusively* pointed Eli out and *exclusively* pointed him out as the antichrist.

By saying what He said, the Lord Jesus was also making it very clear as to who He was literally talking to; yes, He certainly was. In fact, He, while nailed to the cross, personally addressed Eli by literally saying his name, and He even said it twice! Oh, yes He did! Man, can you believe *that?* That is just awesome! That is just amazing! Obviously, the Lord Jesus said Eli's name twice to make it abundantly clear to all that were listening that it was none other than *Eli* who He was speaking to; that's why the Lord Jesus said Eli's name twice. Eli, most definitely, was the person that He was speaking to; it was Eli and absolutely *no one* else. So, what's the reason why I get excited when I think of this one awesome and amazing biblical truth? Well, simply because the Lord Jesus absolutely called out to Eli, the Lord Jesus *absolutely* said Eli's name, even saying it twice, and the Lord Jesus *unquestionably* identified Eli as the antichrist.

Well, one might say, "Yeah, but even though the Lord Jesus did say Eli's name, how is it that He identified him as the antichrist?" My response is this: He identified Eli as the antichrist by simply calling his name; yep, that's right. By simply crying out, "...ELI, ELI..," the Lord Jesus clearly and positively identified Eli as the antichrist; it's just that simple. Seriously, if your neighbor is named, "Ted," don't you call him "Ted," or do you call him, "Billy?" Alright, well, the Lord Jesus said, "...ELI,ELI..," because that's *exactly* who He was specifically addressing when He said, "...ELI, ELI..."

Now, another way how the Lord Jesus positively identified Eli as the antichrist is by the meaning of "...LAMA SABACHTHANI." Those words are Aramaic in nature and as Matthew already has told us, they mean "...why have you forsaken me?" Alright, I now have a question for you: Did Eli forsake the Lord? Yes! *Yes,* Eli forsook the Lord! He absolutely did! Why do you think the Lord Jesus specifically said that? The Lord Jesus said, "...why have you forsaken me?" because Eli *really did* forsake the Lord, and all of the scriptures that have been presented to you thus far in this very book completely and totally prove it! For those of you who don't remember what the scriptures say regarding Eli's personal forsaking of the Lord, here, now, are some questions just for you: You don't remember the man of God that was deliberately sent by the Lord Himself to inform Eli of his upcoming and well-deserved judgment that was due because of his selfish choice to willfully sin? You don't remember that? You don't remember the death judgment that literally fell on Eli's sons because of the sin that Eli was not only responsible for but also personally allowed and approved? You don't remember that? You don't remember Eli being slain with the deadly wound that is spoken of in Revelation 13, the catastrophic and deadly wound that has since been entirely proven to be that of a deadly stroke? You don't remember *that?* You don't remember that God purposely symbolized Eli as the unredeemed ass in Exodus 13, proving *completely* that Eli was *not at all* redeemed by God's holy Lamb and is, in fact, currently burning and being painfully tormented in the Bottomless Pit of Hell? You don't remember that? You don't remember that Eli had his neck violently broken because God chose not to personally redeem him, knowing full well that Eli would never humble himself, never be reconciled to Him but would eventually one day actually become the antichrist? You don't remember *that?* Look, I apologize for being so direct and brutally honest, but it's just that with the Lord Jesus literally saying, "…ELI, ELI..," the undeniable truth is totally overwhelming and clear as crystal; and that truth is this: The Lord Jesus said, "…ELI, ELI…" because that's exactly who He was speaking to – Eli, *exactly!* No, don't make any mistake about it: When the Lord Jesus cried out in a loud voice, "…ELI, ELI…why hast thou forsaken me?" it was because Eli really *did* forsake the Lord as a Levitical Priest, and, consequently, it was very obviously Eli who the Lord was unquestionably addressing – hence, "…ELI, ELI…"

Another way how the Lord Jesus identified Eli as the antichrist is by a truth that has already been revealed to you, and that truth is the actual definition of Eli's name; it means "lofty," remember? It does not mean – I repeat – it does not mean, "My God." No, it absolutely does not. Once again: *it does not mean "My God."* It means "lofty." So, when the Lord Jesus cried out, "…ELI, ELI..," He *meant* Eli; He did *not mean* God or, for that matter, anyone else; no, He did not, and God was *definitely not* who He was speaking to. The fact of the matter is that the Lord Jesus said, "…ELI, ELI…" because He *meant* Eli, and it is just absolutely impossible for God to actually be the One who the Lord Jesus was speaking to when He cried out "…ELI, ELI.." because Eli's name doesn't mean "My God" but means, rather, "lofty." Furthermore, if the Lord Jesus truly meant God (Although, that is definitely difficult to believe because the Lord Jesus is perfect, and this includes when He was speaking to people and calling them by their respective names.) when He cried out to the person with the name "...ELI, ELI..," then He would have just said one of God's actual names, names known throughout the scriptures to, in fact, be names of God like Elohim, for example, or even just one of the names that He mostly used to address God, the Father which was simply "Father."

You see, you have to understand that all of the scriptures, all of theinsight – everything – everything contained in this book that has or will be revealed first graciously originated from God and not me. It has all come from Him, all of it; so, that fact coupled with the true reality of the Lord Jesus publicly and specifically identifying Eli as the antichrist by literally calling out his very name – "...ELI, ELI..." – only indisputably proves that the Lord Jesus was clearly identifying Eli as the antichrist. Furthermore, all of the scriptural evidence as well as everything else that has been revealed to you in this book only points to one person in particular, and that one person is, in fact, Eli. Now, having said that, who else do you know of besides Eli that perfectly fits the following Ellic (antichrist) clues:

- The antichrist is a Jewish Priest.
- The antichrist is so arrogant and filled with pride that he will seek to be called, "God" and even

worshiped as Him (Remember, Hannah and her beautiful prayer were used to establish and, more importantly, prove not only that Eli possesses this lofty trait, but also that he really is the antichrist. She said:

"Talk no more so exceeding proudly;
Let not arrogancy come out of your
Mouth;"
1 Samuel 2: 3

- The antichrist suffered a deadly wound by God as a result of judicial punishment.
- The antichrist died as a result from suffering a deadly wound which was totally proven earlier to unquestionably be a medical stroke which, by the way, specifically takes place in the head – amazing!
- The antichrist's neck was personally broken by God who chose not to personally redeem him; and in the process, the antichrist became a symbolic picture of the unredeemed ass spoken of in Exodus 13.
- As of 95 A.D., the antichrist has already lived *and* died.

See, like I said, there is just no one else that these Ellic clues either point to or fit – period. Look, here: Eli is the antichrist, and that is why the Lord Jesus personally and publicly called him out on that old rugged cross before He lovingly died for you and me. Plus, when you compile not just these major clues but also all of the other ones that have thus far been revealed in this God-inspired, God-ordained book along with the amazing fact that the Lord Jesus actually pointed out just who His future imposter will be by saying, "...ELI, ELI," there is just simply no other person living or otherwise that even remotely has any possible chance whatsoever of fitting all of the Ellic clues; nope, not even one.

Lastly, the simple, mere fact of the Lord Jesus actually causing this very book to be written further demonstrates and proves even the more that He was truly identifying Eli as the antichrist. How? Well, just think about it for a second. The holy Lord has always known that Eli is the antichrist. So, that is why He had all the Ellic clues written in His holy word, why He ordained and exclusively ordered that this book be written, irrefutably identifying Eli as the antichrist, and why He also did everything that He possibly could do for man to fully understand (and not doubt) that the antichrist is, in fact,

Eli, so that, hopefully, no one – I repeat – no one would make the deadly mistake of not positively identifying Eli as the antichrist. Oh, make no mistake about it: The Lord Jesus did not want anyone to not understand in any way that Eli is the antichrist; no, He sure doesn't. The truth is that He unquestionably wants everyone to know that Eli is the antichrist; that's why He, again, specifically pointed out Eli as the antichrist through the Ellic clues that are written in His holy word, why He ordered this book to be written, and why He exclusively and personally identified Eli as His personal imposter while on the cross by saying, "…ELI, ELI…why have you forsaken me?"

One more thing: God wanted this book to be written to serve as a very real warning, a warning of the coming antichrist – Eli – who will one day in the future deceitfully proclaim and represent himself as "God," and who will, if you are not supernaturally raptured by the Good Shepherd when He comes for His sheep, proudly and happily welcome your praise and your devoted worship to him with open arms, as you humble yourself before him in his devilish presence by bowing down on your knees with three sixes tattooed on your forehead.

You know, I got to say something: Quite honestly, with Jesus being on the cross and publicly saying Eli's name coupled together with all the amazing and unbelievable evidence that has been presented thus far in this chapter alone, well, in a courtroom of the law, Eli would no doubt be quickly declared guilty as sin! Yes, he would! On what basis? Well, on the very real and damning basis of witness testimony. Yes, Eli wouldn't stand a chance at ever succeeding in a legal case like the one we have here with the Lord Jesus, and it would all be because of the Lord Jesus's critical statement as a key witness where He actually states both clearly and emphatically Eli's name not only one time *but two,* along with the incredible, overwhelming, and damning evidence that has been methodically and convincingly presented to you thus far.

Alright, here's a question for you: Who knows that when someone verbally cries out to God or speaks to Him directly a prayer is being made? Who knows that? Well, the reason why I ask is because within the Books of Matthew, Mark, Luke, and John, the Lord Jesus prayed a total of 13 prayers (some were repeated) and not once – not even one time – did He ever – I mean, *ever* -- refer to God, the Father as "My God;" nope, He sure didn't, not even once. The fact of the matter is when the Lord Jesus spoke or prayed to God, the Father, He literally called Him "Father." He did not *ever* call Him "My God." Now, He did one time refer to God as "My God (John 20: 17)," but He never *directly called Him* that name (That, by the way, is a *big* difference.); and, for the record, the reason why He referred to God as "My God," is because as a human being living on Planet Earth, He was the Son of Man; and because He was the Son of Man, His God was the heavenly Father, just like the heavenly Father is your God if you are His precious child; so, likewise, you, too, would also refer to God as "My God" exactly like the Jesus did. However, the truth still remains, and boy, is it big, tall, and invincible: While on the cross, the Lord Jesus did not say "My God, My God…" No, He did not. What He did say was, "…ELI, ELI…" *Those* were His words; *those* were the exact words that He spoke, and Eli was unquestionably the person that He was literally speaking to.

Now, regarding those 13 prayers (the prayers of the Lord Jesus where He never referred to the Father as "My God"), the following scriptural references prove it all:

> "…I come to thee, Holy Father…"
> John 17: 11

"O righteous Father..."
John 17: 25

"And he [the Lord Jesus] said, Abba,
Father."
Mark 14: 36

See, the Lord Jesus never – I repeat – never called the Father anything else but either "Father" or "Father" with a complimentary adjective. In fact, His disciples at one time weren't too sure just how to correctly pray to God, so He taught them. Well, at this point, I now have a quick question: Did the Lord Jesus teach His disciples to address God in prayer by calling Him, "My God" or "Eli," for that matter?" If you answered, "No," then you are absolutely right, because the absolute truth is that when He taught the disciples how to pray, He told them to specifically address the Father as "Father" and not "My God" or "Eli." Yep, He sure did, and here's the proof:

"After this manner therefore pray ye:
Our Father..."
Matthew 6: 9

See, the Lord Jesus never told them to pray or speak to their Father by calling Him "My God" or "Eli." He told them to call their God "Father." Why? Well, that's because a Father is who He is to all of His children. Sure, He's God, and sure He's their God, but the Lord Jesus explicitly told them to call their God "Father" and definitely not "My God" or "Eli." So, having said that, why then would he not lead by example and call the Father "…ELI, ELI..?" No, that doesn't make any sense whatsoever, absolutely no sense at all. The truth of the matter is that the Lord Jesus said, "…ELI, ELI…" because that's *exactly* who He was speaking to.

So, having stated all these biblical and historical facts, don't you see the obvious truth? You should. The truth is so incredibly obvious, it's like an image of a big elephant is clearly as well as boldly etched with the use of sequenced dashes right on the face of this very page! I'm serious; it really is that obvious. Look, the obvious truth is that when the Lord Jesus cried out, "…ELI, ELI..," He was not speaking to God but to Eli. Seriously, you find it *anywhere* in the Holy Bible where God is referred to as, "Eli" or that God's name literally means "Eli," and then it'll be true that the Lord Jesus was calling out to God when He cried, "…ELI, ELI;" but guess what? You can't.

No, trust me. You *can't*, and neither can anyone else. Why? Well, for starters, it's just simply impossible; that's right; it's impossible. Why? Well, because it simply is just not the truth. Look, the reality is this: Not any – no, not even one -- of God's many names are titled, "Eli," and not one of His many names literally mean, "Eli." Therefore, the true reality of just who the Lord Jesus was really speaking to when He said, "…ELI, ELI…" while on the cross is, once again, rather quite clear and obvious. The Lord Jesus when on the cross cried, "…ELI, ELI…" because that's exactly who he was speaking to and definitely not God.

Ok, having said that, I now have a question for you: Do you know that absolutely no where in the Holy Bible did the Lord Jesus ever – I mean, ever -- refer to God, the Father as "Eli?" Do you know that? Well, if you don't, you definitely need to because that is 100% the truth – 100%! For the record: The Lord Jesus Christ never – I mean, never – called the Father, "Eli" while in prayer or other-wise. No, not once, not even one, single time. So, with that said, here's another question: Why then would He refer to His Father all of a sudden and totally out of nowhere – literally no where else in the entirety of the Holy Bible – as "Eli?" Why would He do that? No, that just doesn't make any sense, any sense at all. No, the truth of the matter is really quite clear, and it is this: The reason why the Lord Jesus cried out, "…ELI, ELI…" is because He was literally referring to Eli and not His Father; that's the truth; that's what really happened, and let it be factually known: The Lord Jesus when crying out with a loud voice, "…ELI, ELI…" was actually speaking to none other than Eli – hence, "…ELI, ELI…"

Ok, another interesting piece of historical and biblical evidence that also further proves that the Lord Jesus was only speaking to Eli when He said, "…ELI, ELI..," is this verse right here:

> "My God, my God, why hast thou
> Forsaken me?"
> Psalm 22: 1

So, do you see the obvious difference in what this verse says versus what the Lord Jesus *actually did say?* Do you see by what the Lord Jesus actually said as opposed to what this verse says proves even the more that the Lord Jesus was really speaking to Eli and not the Father as some erroneously believe? Do you? The point is this: In that verse you just read, King David is speaking; those are his words. They are not the Lord Jesus'. No, they are not. In fact, we already know what the exact words of the Lord Jesus were; they were these right here:

> "…ELI, ELI, LAMA SABACHTHANI?"
> Matthew 27: 46

See, so, there absolutely is a complete distinction between the two sayings. On one hand David said, "My God, My God," and on the other, the Lord Jesus said, "…ELI, ELI…" I think it's fair to say that if the Lord Jesus wanted to somehow for some reason replicate what David said, He no doubt could have and would have; but He didn't, so, obviously, one clear conclusion can only be made, and that is this: The Lord Jesus made His choice as to who He wanted to personally address, and, without a doubt, it was Eli – hence, "…ELI, ELI…"

Well, I now have a question to ask: Is not the Lord Jesus God (For those of you who incorrectly believe that He is not, perhaps you should look up the following scriptures: John 1:1; Hebrews 1: 1-13)? Ok, and He's perfect too, right? Alright, so, if He truly meant or literally was calling God, the Father when He said, "…ELI, ELI..," then you – those that disagree with the obvious truth of the Lord Jesus calling out to Eli by literally saying, "…ELI, ELI…"

– are calling Him imperfect and mistake prone; yes, you are; that's what you're saying. Look, I don't know about your "god," but *my* God, *my* Jesus, has never made a mistake, and He never will. He doesn't make slip-ups, and He's not full of errors, and He definitely can say a person's name correctly. So, if my Jesus specifically meant to speak to God, the Father, He *for a fact* would have said, "Father" just like He did so many times previously; and He sure wouldn't have called Him, "…ELI, ELI…" Sorry, but that just flat-out doesn't make *any* sense whatsoever and, more importantly, does not hold up in any way against the evidence that clearly and conclusively attests to exactly who and what the Lord Jesus actually did say when He said, "…ELI, ELI…"

Oh, but I can already hear someone saying, "Yeah, but if the Lord Jesus doesn't make mistakes, then who did, and why does it say that He was addressing God, the Father?" Well, I would first like to say that question is a very viable question, and I actually have not just one answer but two answers. Here they are: The simple answer to that question is that Matthew and Mark (His version is located at 15: 34.) just simply didn't know that Eli is the antichrist; and that shouldn't come as no surprise, because up until the summer of 2008, no one did. Evidently, both Matthew and Mark were familiar with Psalm 22, the psalm we looked at earlier, and they very obviously thought that since Psalm 22 is similar in nature and actually does say, "My God, My God," then the Lord Jesus must've been quoting Psalm 22 and was, therefore, speaking to God, the Father, even though the Lord Jesus *did not say,* "My God." So, that's why Matthew and Mark wrote what they wrote; that's why they evidently *felt* that the Lord Jesus meant to say, "…My God, My God…" and was speaking to God, the Father when in all actuality of truthfulness, the Lord Jesus did neither. For the record, when the Lord Jesus said, "…ELI, ELI..," He neither meant to speak to God, nor did He – hence, "…ELI, ELI…"

You know, I got to say this: Perhaps both Matthew and Mark suffered from a faulty memory or maybe after reading the very first verse of Psalm 22, they stopped. Why do I say that? Well, simply because exactly 23 verses later, the psalm clearly states that God *did not* forsake His Son by hiding His face from Him. Yes, it really does say that. Here, you take a look:

> "For he [the Father] hath not despised
> Nor abhorred the affliction of the afflicted;
> Neither hath he hid his face from him [Jesus],

But when he cried unto him, he heard."
Psalm 22: 24

The final answer I have to that probable question is this: Evidently, Matthew and Mark were simply wrong (I say, "were wrong" because now that they're both in Heaven and do not see Eli there with them, they now know the truth of him not just being the antichrist but also of him burning in the pit of Hell.); that's right; they were simply and obviously wrong; and, really, it's not that difficult to understand why they were wrong. Why do I say that? Oh, that's simple. Just look at their reason and even their very, own words for why they say that the Lord Jesus was addressing God, the Father when He specifically said, "… ELI, ELI;" it's wrong! It's all wrong! How? Well, they said that "…ELI, ELI…being interpreted…" "…is to say, My God, My God," *but* we already know and, more importantly, it has already been 100% proven that the name "Eli" *does not mean* My God; no, it does not. What it means is "lofty." So, if you just look at their very, own words, it's rather quite easy to see where and how they actually erred.

Well, guess what? Boy, have I got another juicy tidbit for you! What would you say if I were to tell you that Matthew incorrectly assuming and speaking for the Lord

Jesus was not the only time that he erred when writing his book? Yep, that's right. Matthew committed yet *another* error, and here it is:

> "Then Judas, which had betrayed him,
> When he saw that he was condemned,
> Repented himself, and brought again the
> Thirty pieces of silver to the chief priests
> And elders, Saying, I have sinned in that I
> Have betrayed the innocent blood. And
> They said, What I that to us? See thou to
> That. And he cast down the pieces of silver
> In the temple, and departed, and went and
> Hanged himself. And the chief priests took
> The silver pieces, and said, It is not lawful for
> To put them into the treasury, because it is
> The price of blood. And they took counsel,
> And bought with them the potter's field, to
> Bury strangers in. Wherefore that field was
> Called, The field of blood, unto this day. Then
> Was fulfilled that which was spoken by Jeremy
> The prophet, saying, And they took the thirty
> Pieces of silver, the price of him that was
> Valued, whom they of the children of Israel
> Did value: And they gave them for the potter's

Field, as the Lord appointed me."
Matthew 27: 3-10

So, did you happen to notice Matthew's second error? Did you? If not, that's Ok. Here's a hint: The error is towards the end of the passage. Do you see it now? Matthew's error was when he incorrectly stated that the Prophet Jeremiah was the one who wrote, "And they took the thirty pieces of silver, the price of him that was valued, whom they of the children of Israel did value: And they gave them for the potter's field, as the Lord appointed me." That is his second error, and from the looks of it, it appears Matthew was actually paraphrasing. Nevertheless, it wasn't the Prophet Jeremiah who said that verse. It was the Prophet Zechariah who did. Oh, you want to see the proof, huh? Ok, here it is:

> "And I said unto them, if ye think good, give
> Me my price; and if not, forbear, So they
> Weighed for my price thirty pieces of silver.
> And the Lord said unto me, Cast it unto the
> Potter: a goodly price that I was prised at
> Of them. And I took the thirty pieces of
> Silver, and cast them to the potter in the

House of the Lord."
Zechariah 11: 12-13

See, Zechariah really did write that passage, and this error just proves even the more as well as totally cements the already proven, iron-clad fact that when Matthew and Mark, for that matter, wrongly assumed that the Lord Jesus was speaking to God, the Father when He was actually speaking to Eli, they were totally 100% incorrect; and all of the amazing scriptural evidence that has been presented thus far overwhelmingly proves this indisputable truth to be beyond any measure of any reasonable doubt. As I have heard someone say many times before, "Put it down big, plain, and straight:" Matthew and Mark were completely wrong in assuming that the Lord Jesus was speaking to God, the Father when He was really and truthfully speaking directly to the Curse of the Levitical Priests, the antichrist, Eli – hence, "…ELI, ELI…"

So, the question for you is this: Why in the world would you choose to believe Matthew and Mark's erroneous interpretation? I mean, seriously, the evidence *overwhelmingly* shows that not only was both of their interpretations actual assumptions at best, but they are also entirely incorrect. Look, the evidence speaks for itself and is really quite clear. It undeniably states that when the Lord Jesus "…cried out in a loud voice, saying ELI, ELI LAMA SABACHTHANI..," He was literally crying out to none other than the person whose very name that He spoke; and that one and only person without question is the antichrist, the symbolized and unredeemed ass, Eli.

Well, guess what else? Matthew and Mark weren't the only ones to write erroneous assumptions based off of their own, personal feelings in God's word; nope, they sure weren't (Ok, you can manually close your mouth with your hands as well as fix your eyes back to their normal, open position.). Why do I say that? Well, as it turns out, the Apostle Paul, too, was also wrong by personally assuming things and including them in the scriptures; yep, he, too, was totally incorrect in what he *assumed* to be the truth, but really, for all intents and purposes, it wasn't the truth at all. Now, having said that, here is the very proof of what I'm saying, the literal proof of Paul also assuming personal and incorrect beliefs and writing them down in God's word when they, in fact, are absolutely not the truth at all:

> "Behold, I shew you a mystery: We shall
> Not all sleep, but we shall all be changed,

In a moment, in the twinkling of an eye,
At the last trump: for the trumpet shall
Sound, and the dead shall be raised
Incorruptible, and we shall be changed."
1 Corinthians 15: 51-52

"…we which are alive and remain unto the
Coming of the Lord shall not prevent them
Which are asleep…then we which are alive
And remain shall be caught up together with
Them in the clouds…"
1 Thessalonians 4: 15, 17

What we have here in these two passages prove so many different things, but please allow me to first explain them. Both of these passages are written by Paul, both revolve around the Rapture, and both definitively show how he wrongly assumed that he and his fellow saints would still be alive one day on earth when the Lord Jesus comes down from Heaven and supernaturally raptures His children up into the clouds. Needless to say, what Paul *assumed* did not happen. "So, what's the point," someone might ask. Well, the point is that just like Matthew and Mark were wrong, so was Paul. The good news is that although Matthew, Mark, and Paul were allowed by God to include their personal commentary and wrong assumptions in The Holy Bible, it doesn't change a thing. How? Well, simply by the fact that even though Paul was, indeed, wrong in assuming that he would one day witness the Rapture and be an actual participant, the Rapture still is going to happen one day. Likewise, even though both Matthew and Mark were totally wrong in assuming that the Lord Jesus was talking to God, the Father when in all actuality, He was *really* speaking to Eli, it doesn't matter one bit. Why? Well, simply because Eli is *still* the antichrist. Plus, the Lord Jesus has already both shown *and* proved that Eli really is the Man of Sin in His word, even saying his very own name – "…ELI, ELI,…" Additionally, the Lord also gave us The Holy Bible to conclusively see for ourselves that Eli really is the antichrist, and last but not least, God, once again, deliberately caused this very book to be written, telling, explaining, and even undeniably proving to the entirety of the mankind that the antichrist is none other than Eli; and, in the process, He completely debunked and corrected both Matthew and Mark's wrong assumptions that incorrectly stated the Lord Jesus was speaking to God, the Father when He was actually speaking to that loser, Eli – hence, "… ELI, ELI…"

On a side note, God obviously did not want the world to know until now that Eli is, in fact, the antichrist. I say that because if He really did want the world to know sooner, then He wouldn't have allowed Matthew and Mark to incorrectly state that the Lord Jesus was calling out to God, the Father when He was really calling Eli. He also would have only allowed them to stick to the facts of what actually transpired; and what are the facts? Oh, that's simple. The facts are that the Lord Jesus actually said, "…ELI, ELI…" and was, therefore, only referring to Eli and absolutely no one else – hence, "…ELI, ELI…"

Alright, what I'd like to discuss now is this: I am well aware of how just about everyone under the sun wrongly believes that God, the Father actually abandoned the Lord Jesus while on the cross. I am also aware of why they, unfortunately, believe this inaccurate idea. They believe it primarily because of Matthew and Mark's incorrect assumptions, stating that the name "Eli" means "My God" when, in fact, it actually means "lofty." Well, I just want it to be *very clear* that God, the Father *never left* the Lord Jesus – no, not even onetime -- and here, now, is the proof:

> "And yet if I [the Lord Jesus] judge, my
> Judgment is true: for I am not alone, but

I and the Father that sent me."
John 8: 16

"Jesus answered them Do ye believe now?
Behold, the hour cometh, yea, is now come,
That ye shall be scattered, every man to
His own, and shall leave me alone: and yet
I am not alone, because the Father is with
Me."
John 16: 31-32

"And he [the Father] that sent me [the
Lord Jesus] is with me: the Father hath
Not left me alone, for I do always those
Things that please him."
John 8: 29

All three of those supporting references prove without a doubt that the Father was *always* with His Son, Jesus, and that He never, ever deserted Him; but what I think is the most significant statement made by the Lord Jesus was when He gave the explicit reason for *why* the Father never leaves and is always with Him; He said, "the Father hath not left me alone; for I **do always those things that please him**." See, right there, *right there,* is all the further proof that you need to know for sure that God, the Father never deserted Him. Why do I say that? Well, wasn't it the Father's will for the Lord Jesus to be nailed to that cross? Wasn't it? Ok, and did it not please the Father to purposely send His only son to painfully suffer – even death – on our behalf so that the penalty of sin would be completely paid in full? Ok, and isn't that one of the reasons why the Father willingly sent His only Son in the first place? Alright, well, to be sure, here's the proof that it was, indeed, the Father's will to brutally sacrifice His Son on the cross and that the Father was also thoroughly pleased in doing so:

> "Yet it pleased the Lord [God, the Father] to
> Bruise him [the Lord Jesus]; he [the Father]
> Hath put him to grief: when thou shalt make
> Make his soul an offering for sin, he shall see
> His seed, he shall prolong his days, and the
> Pleasure of the Lord shall prosper in his hand.
> He shall see of the travail of his soul, and shall
> Be satisfied."
> Isaiah 53: 10-11

> "Therefore doth my Father love me, because
> I lay down my life...This commandment have

I received of my Father."
John 10: 17-18

See, God the Father really was entirely pleased with the Lord Jesus when He was sacrificed on a cross. See, He really was! It was also the Father's plan from the beginning, His perfect plan all along! So, since it was the Father's plan all along, and since the Father was absolutely pleased with His Son for always obeying Him, then it is unquestionably true that the Father *never abandoned, never forsook* the Lord Jesus while He was on the cross. No, He absolutely, positively *did not*. The Father was *always* with His Son, always, even while His Son was being sacrificed on the cross. Now, check this out: So, since the Father was with the Lord Jesus while on the cross, then it is just totally impossible that the Lord Jesus was calling out to the Father when He said, "…ELI, ELI..LAMA SABACHTHANI;" that's right; it *couldn't* have been Him – couldn't have been the Father. "Well, if it wasn't Him, then who was it?," someone might say. Oh, that's *real* easy. I'm so happy to tell you who it was! It was the very person that He cried out to, Eli – hence, "…ELI, ELI…"

Now, have I got something for you; and this is a good one! In the following passage, well…uh…I was going to do a little explaining first, but you know what? On second thought, go ahead and read the passage, and then I'll make my comments. Ok? Alright, here it is:

> "And there were also two other, malefactors,
> Led with him [the Lord Jesus] to be put to
> Death. And when they were come to the
> Place which is called Calvary, there they
> Crucified him, and the malefactors, one on
> The right hand, and the other on the left.
> Then said Jesus, Father, forgive them; for
> They know not what they do. And when
> Jesus had cried with a loud voice, he said,
> Father, into thy hands I commend my spirit."
> Luke 23: 32-34; 46

The passage that you just read consists of the actual two prayers that the Lord Jesus prayed to God, the Father while on the cross. Having said that, did you happen to notice that when He prayed those two prayers to God, the Father, He also addressed Him as "Father" *both times?* Yeah, He certainly did! Oh, but someone might ask, "So, what is so significant about that?" Well, I'll tell you what is so incredibly significant about that. It's the fact that the Lord Jesus did not – I repeat – did not call

Him, "Eli" or "My God." Nope, He sure didn't. He called Him, "Father" and "Father" *both times!* Now, do you see the incredible significance? See, that is why for *anyone* – including the Disciples Matthew and Mark – to suggest, think, or believe that when the Lord Jesus said, "…ELI, ELI.. ("…Eloi, Eloi…" in Mark's personal account – Eli's name in the Greek language)," He was speaking to God, the Father, is not only entirely wrong but their assumption is absolutely ridiculous; it really is. Why? Well, when praying those two prayers on the cross to the Father, did the Lord Jesus ever, one single time call the Father "Eli?" No, He sure didn't. Did He call Him "My God?" Nope, not that name either. Alright, then, as if more biblical and factual proof is needed at this time, it just *couldn't* have been the Father that the Lord Jesus was speaking to when He said, "…ELI, ELI…" Listen, don't make any mistake about it: It couldn't have been, and it absolutely wasn't; it was, however, Eli whom the Lord Jesus was speaking to, and He personally proved it Himself by literally saying Eli's very name, saying, in fact, "…ELI, ELI…" Also (This fact will be extra proof, because I'm not so sure that one would really need it because of all the indisputable proof that has been given thus far.), here's one more factual point: If it was really the Father that the Lord Jesus was calling when He said, "…ELI, ELI..," then why in the world didn't the Lord Jesus call the Father "Eli" when He spoke to Him those other two times while on the cross? Why not those two times *also?* Why all of a sudden and totally out of the blue after calling His Father, "Father," just like He always, in fact, *had done* while walking the very face of this planet, would He now inexplicably refer to Him as, "Eli," a name, mind you, that has been factually, biblically, and even historically documented to *never* have been used by the Lord Jesus not one, single time, and also a name that, may I remind you, does not mean by definition anything even remotely close to any of the Father's actual names? See, it just doesn't make any sense, any sense whatsoever that the Lord Jesus was speaking to the Father or anyone else, for that matter, other than that loser Eli when He said, "…ELI, ELI…" Listen up: The unquestionable truth of the matter is that when the Lord Jesus said, "…ELI, ELI..," Eli was the one and only person who He was speaking to, and Eli was also the only one who personally forsook Him by foolishly choosing to one day become that cursed beast, Leviathan, the Curse of the Levitical Priests, the antichrist – hence, "…ELI, ELI…why hast thou forsaken me?"

Ok, so, there's a verse that I have seen mentioned and improperly used while the Lord Jesus was on the cross.

It was used in the sense to supposedly prove (insert laugh here) that God, the Father really did turn away from the Lord Jesus, because the Father just couldn't bear to see the Lord Jesus with His own eyes due to the Lord Jesus bearing the sin of mankind while on the cross. Well, first of all, that belief is totally absurd. Nevertheless, here's the verse:

> "Thou [You, God] art of purer eyes than to
> Behold evil, and canst not look on iniquity:
> Wherefore lookest thou upon them that deal
> Treacherously…"
> Habakkuk 1: 13

The true meaning of this verse is found in the actual Hebraic definition of the word, "look." It's true meaning by implication is to "…regard with pleasure, favor, or care."[25] Now, come on. Who doesn't know that the Father cannot look favorably on iniquity? Who doesn't know that? Alright, who doesn't know that the Father cannot look at iniquity in a pleasurable way? Ok, and lastly, who doesn't know that it is impossible for the Father to view or look at sin in any way with approval or care? Who doesn't know that? *Of*

---

[25] Ibid., 90

course, the Father cannot look at sin with favor in His eyes, pleasure in His mind, or approval or care in His heart – of course He can't. To say that He does, would not only be nonsensical but also blasphemous! So, having said that, the true meaning and the factual point that I would now like to make is this: Since the Father does, indeed, look at the sinful acts of humanity (and even records them in a book; Revelation 20: 12) with total disapproval and sadness, then He most definitely looked down from Heaven and saw His Son bearing the sin of the world while on the cross who, I might add, *totally* pleased Him by not just being completely obedient by doing everything that He was asked to do, but, more importantly, by also perfectly fulfilling the very purpose, reason, and plan for why He was sent to earth in the first place; and in the process, the Lord Jesus humbly caused the Father to pleasingly hear the very proof of His total obedience by hearing His Son say the following three words: "It is finished [John 19: 30]." No, don't make any mistake about it: The Father *never* forsook the Lord Jesus, and because He didn't, it wasn't the Father who Jesus was speaking to when He said, "…ELI, ELI…" Who was it? Oh, that's simple. It was Eli – hence, "…ELI, ELI…"

Ok, I'm about to show you a very small verse. It's one you actually have seen already, but it's of huge significance because in it, Eli is personally addressed by God. Yep, I tell you no lie. Eli really is addressed by God, and here it is:

> "But ye are they that forsake the Lord
> That forget my holy mountain, that
> Prepare a table for that troop, and
> That furnish the drink offering unto
> That number."
> Isaiah 65: 11

So, did you happen to notice the first eight words that God spoke to Eli? Did you? God said to him, "But ye are they that forsake the Lord…" See, if you ever needed any more proof (which I don't know why you would, seeing that all of the factual evidence that has been presented so far is, at this point, *completely* overwhelming) of Eli forsaking the Lord Jesus and knowing for sure -- 100% even – that it *really was Eli* who the Lord Jesus was speaking to when He said, "…ELI, ELI..," then you were just now given it; that's right; you certainly were. Here, in this passage, the holy Lord speaks directly to Eli and even proclaims with no uncertainty whatsoever that Eli absolutely forsook Him. Whoa! How about *that?* That's incredible! See, I told you. I told you that this juicy tidbit really ought to be all you'll ever need to fully know in your heart of hearts that Eli really did forsake the Lord; and it also ought to be the very last nail in the coffin, so to speak, that ultimately causes you to know for a certainty that it was absolutely Eli – and only Eli – who the Lord Jesus was speaking to when He said, "…ELI, ELI…"

Now, do I have something special for you! Yep, I certainly do, and it is this: What would you say if I were to ask, "Would you now like to witness for yourself the amazing, literal proof of the Lord Jesus not only paying mankind's sin-debt, but actually observe Him paying it while being nailed to a cross through the amazing, revelatory eyes of symbolism, symbolism that was deliberately and secretly hidden away in the scriptures by the awesome God?" Well, would you? Wait! Hold on! Don't answer yet! It's about to get even better! Alright, here's another question: What would you say if I were to tell you that through that same, incredible, symbolic proof of Jesus actually paying mankind's sin-debt, you will also exclusively witness not only the already proven truth of God, the Father never – no, no ever – forsaking the Lord Jesus while on the cross, but also at the very same time, you'll amazingly observe the also already proven truth that very clearly declares that it really was Eli who Jesus was directly speaking to when He, "…cried with a loud voice, saying, ELI, ELI LAMA SABACHTHANI?" Well, you can now go ahead and give me an answer, because here is that incredible, symbolic proof:

> "Then came Amalek, and fought with Israel
> In Rephidim. And Moses said unto Joshua,
> Choose us out men, and go out, fight with
> Amalek: to morrow I will stand on the top
> Of the hill with the rod of God in mine hand.
> So Joshua did as Moses had said to him, and
> Fought with Amalek: and Moses, Aaron, and
> Hur went up to the top of the hill. And it
> Came to pass, when Moses held up his hand,
> That Israel prevailed: and when he let down
> His hand Amalek prevailed. But Moses
> Hands were heavy; and they took a stone,
> And put it under him, and he sat thereon;
> And Aaron and Hur stayed up his hands,
> The one on the one side, and the other on
> The other side; and his hands were steady
> Until the going down of the sun. And Joshua
> Discomforted Amalek and his people with
> The edge of the sword."
> Exodus 17: 8-13

So, did you observe all that astonishing symbolism I spoke of earlier? Did you? Did you symbolically see the Lord Jesus on the cross, paying mankind's very own sin-debt that was due? Did you? Did you witness for yourself the absolute truth of God, the Father never, ever – *ever*, for that matter – forsaking His glorious Son while He was being crucified on the cross? Did you? Lastly, after witnessing for yourself all that amazing, symbolic evidence (if, in fact, you did), did you correctly conclude that it really was *Eli* whom the Lord Jesus was specifically calling out to when He "...cried with a loud voice, saying, ELI, ELI LAMA SABACHTHANI?" Did you? Well, the reason why I ask these extremely important questions is because the fact of the matter is that through the eyes of the Holy Ghost symbolism, the Lord Jesus is literally seen paying for everyone's own personal debt of sin through the patriarch Moses; yep, this is true; it really is. You see, in the person of Moses, particularly with Moses holding up his arms, the Lord Jesus is being symbolically represented on the cross; He really is (John 19: 18)! Isn't that just amazing? It certainly is amazing! Oh, but the symbolism doesn't end there. There's more, much more, truly unforgettable and amazing symbolism, and here, now, is the rest: The Amalekites, the group of people that the Israelites were fighting, symbolically represent the dark, evil, spiritual forces that everyone battles against (whether they know it or not; 1 Corinthians 2: 4-8; Colossians 2: 15), and Aaron and Hur are also personally symbolized within this holy passage; they symbolically represent the two thieves (Luke 23: 32-33) that were also crucified alongside the Lord Jesus, one being to the right of the Redeeming Lamb of God and the other one on His opposite side; and get this: Just like in the historical case with the Lord Jesus, there is also only one person of those two men (Aaron and Hur) who was allowed into Paradise, and that one and only person (in my humble opinion) is Aaron (Luke 23: 40-43; Deuteronomy 32: 48-50) and unquestionably not Hur (Luke 23: 39). "Why Aaron?" someone might ask. Well, simply because no one back in the times when Moses was alive whose name means what Hurs actually does (Remember, the meaning of names back then were highly significant and meant literally everything. We already established this irrefutable truth in the first chapter.) *ever* got to feast their eyes on those glorious and indescribably beautiful streets of gold – no one! Oh, so right about now you most definitely would like to know just exactly what Hur's name means, wouldn't you? I don't blame you. I would want to know what it means right now too if I were you. Well, good thing for you, I looked it up, and believe it or not, part of the literal meaning of his very name is "…the crevice of a serpent…the cell of a prison."[26] Wow! See, I told you! I told you biblical names have extraordinary meaning! So, like I said, Aaron's *definitely* the one out of him and Hur who made it into Paradise. It should also be mentioned that all three of them – Moses, Aaron, and Hur – were on a hill just like the Lord Jesus was with those two thieves when He lovingly died a very vicious death for you and I (Luke 23: 33). Wow, God's word is truly one of a kind, totally alive, and absolutely fantastic! God is also the best author ever!

Well, as if it couldn't get any better than it already is (and, believe me, it's certainly about to get a whole *lot* better by way of more shocking, eye-opening, incredible truths – truths that have never been revealed , and truths that are now only being revealed because of the Lord Jesus Himself – that are, once again, going to blow the socks right off your feet, make your hair stand straight up no matter how curly it may be, and open your mouth so wide that all you'll be able to see is the outside of your upper lip.), there are still many more symbolic points left to be made regarding this outstanding, symbolic passage God

---

[26] Ibid., 41

graciously gave to us. The first point is this one right here: Earlier, I asked the question, "Did you witness for yourself the absolute truth of God, the Father never, ever – *ever*, for that matter – forsaking His Son while He was being crucified on the cross?" Well, the reason why I asked that question is because not only is what I'm implying the actual, wholehearted truth, but, more importantly, the irrefutable evidence of God never forsaking His Son can be literally and unquestionably seen with what Moses was holding in his very own hand; yep, that's right; it certainly can be seen, and what did Moses have in his hand, completely proving beyond the shadow of any reasonable doubt, that God *never* forsook His Son, the Lord Jesus Christ? What was it? Well, as a matter of historical and symbolic fact, Moses had none other than "…the rod of God," *one of the articles symbolizing the very presence of God Himself;* and get this: It was with Moses! That's right; it was *with Moses! It was with Moses,* in his *very own hand,* and separated from him *not!* Wow! Incredible! The "… rod of God…" symbolizing the Father's very own, actual presence was united with him, together with him, and they were united as one – *exactly* like God, the Father was always with the Lord Jesus and even when He was on that old rugged cross! The Father was with the Lord Jesus while on the cross, and He *never* "left me alone [John 8:

29; 16: 31-32]!" See, I told you God never forsook His Son! See, I told you, and all the more undeniable and irrefutable proof of Him absolutely not forsaking the Lord Jesus while He was on the cross is right there before your very eyes within that outstanding, symbolic passage! See, I told you God never forsook the Lord Jesus, and now you have exclusively been given – by God Himself – the unquestionable, symbolic proof of Him never – no, not *ever!* – forsaking His Son! See, I told you! Wow! Now that is just incredible, absolutely incredible!

Well, at this time, it really ought to be pointed out that the "...rod of God...(again, symbolizing the Father's very own presence)" Moses had in his hand while he symbolically represented the Lord Jesus on the cross is the same, exact "...rod of God..." that was with Moses when he was personally called by God (Exodus 4: 1-3) to deliver God's chosen people from the "...iron furnace, even out of Egypt...[Deuteronomy 4: 20]," the same "... rod of God..." that symbolized God's power and presence and was exclusively used to perform all those trulyawe-inspiring and incredible plagues that were called down upon Pharaoh and the land of Egypt (Exodus 4: 17), the same "...rod of God..." that symbolically represented God's supernatural and unmistakable presence that undeniably was with Moses as he began his journey from Midian with God (Exodus 4: 19-20), the same "… rod of God…" that the awesome God used to display His truly incomparable power and ever loving presence with Moses by miraculously transforming it ("…the rod of God…") into a snake (Exodus 7: 8-9), the same "…rod of God…" that the Almighty God used to totally defeat – and even swallow up – the demonically inspired snakes of the Egyptian sorcerers (Exodus 7: 12), the same "…rod of God…" that the Most High used to incredibly transform the Nile River into blood (Exodus 7: 17), the same "…rod of God…" the Almighty used to also miraculously turn all of the Egyptian streams , rivers, ponds, "…pools of water…" and even "…vessels of wood, and…vessels of stone…" into blood (Exodus 7: 19), the same "…rod of God…" God used to supernaturally cause frogs to come forth the waters of Egypt (Exodus 8: 5), the same "…rod of God…" that God used to display His awesome power and undeniable presence by commanding a multitude of gnats to infest Egypt (Exodus 8: 16-17), the same "…rod of God…" God used to violently rain down lightning, thunder, and hail all across the land where the Egyptian's dwelt (Exodus 9: 23), the same "…rod of God…" the Almighty used to display His amazing power and ever loving presence by causing locusts to totally inhabit and

engulf the land of Egypt (Exodus 10: 12-13), the same "...
rod of God..." the Most High used in order to cause complete darkness all over the land where the Egyptians dwelt
(Exodus 10: 21-22), the same "...rod of God..." that symbolized God's personal presence with the Israelites when
they, as instructed by God Himself, ate their Passover
meal with – you guess it – the "...staff [rod] of God..." in
their hand (Exodus 12: 1, 11), the same "...rod of God..."
that symbolically represented the mighty God's personal
presence and unmatched power by literally splitting the
Red Sea in half (Exodus 14: 15-16; 21-22), the same "...
rod of God..." that was used to not just split the Red
Sea in half, but also was used to completely wipe out
the Egyptians – Israel's enemies – by causing the raging
waters of the Red Sea to come crashing down upon them
(Exodus 14: 26-28), the same "...rod of God..." that symbolically represented God's personal presence and awesome power by miraculously causing water to come out
of a rock located in Rephidim (Exodus 17: 5-6), and last
but definitely not least, the same "...rod of God..." that
was used to symbolically display God's personal presence
and amazing power by, once again, causing water to amazingly come straight out of a rock, this time located in
Kadesh (Numbers 20: 8)." So, the point here that is being
made is through the outstanding, Holy Ghost-inspired

symbolism of Moses holding "...the rod of God..," God is unquestionably saying and 100% proving to us that He, in fact, *was* – I repeat, *was* – with the Lord Jesus while He was suffering on the cross, and that He absolutely, positively, did not in *any way, shape, or form* forsake His holy Son; no, He certainly did not, and all the astonishing proof of Him not forsaking the Lord Jesus is found in that "...rod of God..." being in Moses hand as he symbolically pictured the Lord Jesus being crucified on that mountain top and paying for man's sin-debt on that old rugged cross with the very presence of God, the Father *still* with Him. Now, I must say, that's what I call – in football terms – sidestepping the fierce pass rush of an opposing team, looking down field and finding your favorite wide receiver splitting the double coverage between the safety and the corner, and victoriously throwing a 99 yard touchdown pass! Hallelujah! Praise the Lord!

Alright, it is now time to present another symbolic point; this point was actually presented earlier, but through that outstanding, symbolic passage of Moses actually portraying the Lord Jesus on the cross with the Father *still* – I repeat – *still* with Him, it once again is further proven and should be looked at once more. The point is this: Since it really *is* entirely true and totally irrefutable (especially now with that fantastic, symbolic passage being introduced), that the Father never forsook Jesus while He was on the cross, then, consequently, it is *also* true that when Jesus "…cried out in a loud voice, saying, ELI, ELI LAMASABACHTHANI..," He was crying out to none other than the one person whose very name that He literally spoke, and the name of that one person whose name He literally spoke is none other than the antichrist, the symbolized and unredeemed ass, the stupid ass, Eli. Oh, but someone might ask, "How does it prove that Jesus was speaking to Eli and not God, the Father?" Well, it proves it by "…the rod of God [*the very, symbolic presence of God, the Father Himself, symbolically]…*" actually being with Moses who, again, symbolically pictures Jesus dying for mankind's sins; that's how. See, as I have said all throughout this chapter and, most importantly, how it has now been unquestionably proven *far* beyond a shadow of any reasonable doubt, I'll happily say it one last time: God, the Father never forsook the Lord Jesus while He was on the cross, and all the unconquerable evidence that has been presented within this chapter clearly shows that He didn't; it really does. So, since God never did forsake the Lord Jesus, then it *really was Eli* whom Jesus was directly speaking to when He "…cried out in a loud voice, saying

ELI, ELI LAMA SABACHTHANI…" and absolutely, positively no one else.

If I may, I'd now like to make something very clear, and it is this: I'd like to state that in regards to that truly awesome symbolic passage, the fact that God, the Father, the Lord Jesus, Moses, Aaron, and Hur can all be seen symbolically, it is in no way, shape, or form a false teaching, destructive heresy, or new doctrine; no, it is not, and the very proof of it not being any of those horrible, divisive weapons of Satan, is what is actually *with* Moses and what he is literally holding in his very own hand – the "…rod of God..," the very, may I remind you, symbolic presence of God Himself. Lastly, this wonderful, symbolic theme has always been in The Holy Bible since its initial conception. It was quietly nestled away and secretly hidden within all those other Holy Ghost-inspired words that were most likely physically written by Moses' very own hand (John 5: 46-47).

In light of the awesome, symbolic passage of Exodus 17, I'd now like to make three very important points in regards to Matthew and Mark's erroneous assumptions. They are as follows:

- The "…rod of God…" being in Moses' hand as he symbolically portrays Jesus on the cross totally – I repeat – totally refutes those misguided assumptions of both Matthew and Mark, stating that Jesus was speaking to God when He was *really and truthfully* speaking to the person whose name that He actually said – Eli – saying it, in fact, two, separate times – "…ELI, ELI…" Listen, I've said it all through this chapter, and I'll gladly say it one more time: Matthew and Mark were 100% wrong, and all the incredible, irrefutable evidence that has been presented *in this chapter alone* totally prove this fact.

- Obviously, it is a matter of extreme importance that this truth would now be stated: The "…rod of God…" preceded Matthew and Mark's erroneous assumptions; yes, it certainly did, and that, ladies and gentlemen, is worth it's weight in pure, solid, heavenly gold. Why? Well, simply because – if anything – Matthew and Mark's incorrect guesses are nothing but a new doctrine, false teaching, or divisive heresy. How? Well, firstly, by the simple fact that the symbolism was there *before* Matthew and Mark even opened their mouths or picked up a pen, not to mention the fact that the amazing symbolism actually gives such a clear picture of what really transpired at Calvary, the honest to goodness fact that the Father was always with the Lord Jesus and *never* left His side; that's how.

- Lastly, I think it should be pointed out that evidently Matthew and Mark didn't know of that incredible, symbolic passage. Why do I say that? Well, simply because if they, in fact, *were* aware of it, then they would've never written that ridiculous, unscriptural, and erroneous assumption, stating that the Father forsook His fully obedient Son, who, therefore, completely pleased Him while He was on the cross. "They wouldn't have?" someone might ask. No, they most certainly wouldn't, and the reason why is because what they incorrectly assumed goes completely – *completely*, I say – against what the scriptures already, emphatically state; and what do they state? Well, as a matter of historic and symbolic fact, they (the symbolic scriptures of Exodus 17) wholeheartedly state that the Father ("…the rod of God…") was actually *with* the Lord Jesus (Moses) as He paid for mankind's sin-debt while being crucified on the cross. So, if Matthew and Mark were actually aware of this truly amazing, symbolic passage, then they most definitely wouldn't have wrote what they wrote – that laughable, absurd, and ridiculous assumption incorrectly stating that Jesus was speaking to God when He actually said exactly who He was literally speaking to when He "… cried out in a loud voice, saying, ELI, ELI LAMA SABACHTHANI…" However, I am in no way faulting Matthew and Mark for not being aware of this wonderful, symbolic passage. I am no better than they. I, myself, was completely unaware of all that awesome symbolism hidden away within that particular passage too (and I even read it a few times); that is, until God Himself opened my eyes to it.

Well, that's it for this chapter. Wow, it sure did pack a lot of wonderful truths in it. So that someone's thrilling surprise is not ruined, the next chapter will not include Eli's name. Instead, it will be replaced with "He."

With that, this chapter is done.

Apokalupto

No one knows when it will happen. It could happen many years from now. It could happen sooner, but one thing is for sure: Eli is coming.

The Bible tells us of his coming (1 John 2: 18). No doubt it will surely be an event to see. Fire will rain down from Heaven. Signs and wonders of all kinds will shock the masses. The greatest fireworks show and movie production will be put to shame. Eli will be in full bloom and ready to go. He will be so happy, so content ... *so excited*. His time has finally come, and he's been waiting for so long. His moment is finally here, and he will certainly seize it. Now, he can do what he wants to do. At last, he can be who he's always wanted to be, and the whole world will witness it all.

Yes, indeed, Eli's second arrival on earth will certainly be an amazing spectacle. The looks on people's faces when they see him will say it all. The Apostle Paul in his letter to the Thessalonians mentioned this truth as well, but what I'd like to focus in on now is, actually, just one word that Paul used found in this passage of scripture right here:

> "Now we beseech you, brethren, by the
> Coming of our Lord Jesus Christ, and by
> Our gathering together unto him. That
> Ye be not soon shaken in mind, or be
> Troubled, neither by spirit, or by word,
> Nor by letter as from us, as that the day
> Of Christ is at hand. Let no man deceive
> You by any means; for that day shall not
> Come, except there come a falling away
> First, and that man of sin be revealed…
> And now ye know what withholdeth that
> He might be revealed in his time. For the
> Mystery of iniquity doth already work:
> Only he who now letteh will let, until he
> Be taken out of the way. And then shall
> That wicked be revealed…"
> 2 Thessalonians 2: 1-3; 6-8

So, this passage pretty much revolves around the Rapture and the unforgettable day when Eli will finally be able to experience a supernatural resurrection from the Bottomless Pit of Hell and deceitfully reveal himself to the whole world as a fake god and fake messiah. Where I'd like to comment first is on the word, "revealed." It's a Greek word – apokalupto – and it's meaning among other things is, "…to take off the cover…"[27] Now, I've got to ask a question: Doesn't that sound sort of familiar, even a *little?* If it doesn't, it should. Why? Well, simply because the definition is the very title of this book, and the word itself is the very title of this chapter. Now, the reason why this book is titled that particular definition, is because I wanted to make it very clear as to what Paul *is* saying versus what he is not. So, what Paul is saying is this: When the antichrist (Eli) is seen by becoming visible to the physical eye, *that's when* he will be revealed. In another words, when the cover (Obviously, this "cover" is not literal in nature; it is a figure of speech.) that is presently hiding him (I say, "presently" because as I write this book, no one knows that Eli is the antichrist. The figurative "cover" is still on him and covering his true identity.) is taken off and he is finally seen, that's when he will be

---

[27] Ibid., 11

revealed – hence, "…to take off the cover…" This is exactly what Paul meant and nothing else whenever he used the word, "revealed" in that supporting reference. This is why the actual definition of the word "revealed" means "…to take off the cover..," because it denotes and specifies an action, and one that will result in allowing whatever was previously covered, previously unseen to literally *be seen*. The following statement is a perfect sample of what Paul meant: "And then shall that Wicked be revealed [seen]."

I must be a visual kind of dude, because earlier I gave you a mental example, and I'm about to do it again. Here goes:

Ok, picture in your mind that you're sitting in a beautiful theatre, the most gorgeous theatre you've ever seen in your life. You are there alone. You're sitting in the seventh row from the stage right in the very middle of the theatre. Your view is perfect. The chairs are so magnificent. They are made up of wonderfully engraved oak wood, the color of pure gold and bright red tweeded fabric. The stage rises up around four feet high from the ground, and everything is perfect. You are there because you are calmly waiting to see the star of the show; and he's about to be revealed. In fact, he's right behind the lovely deep maroon, ornate curtains that stand floor to ceiling. They are very tall, around 25 feet in height, and as of yet are not fully drawn. You cannot see the star of the show. He is fully covered and cannot be seen. Ok, it's time. The show will start now, and the star of the show will finally be revealed. Soft music begins to play, but as the curtains are pulled to the sides, the music thunders and you see the star of the show standing directly in front of you! You see him eye to eye, and he also sees you.

Alright, you can come back to reality. The example is over now, but, see, that's exactly what Paul meant when he used the word, "revealed." Unequivocally, Paul meant that the day the antichrist is "revealed" is the day when he is seen. Likewise, when the cover that is hiding the antichrist from being seen is finally taken off, only then will he be revealed for all to see. Now, that's *exactly* what the Apostle Paul meant when he used the word, "revealed."

Now, conversely, what Paul is not saying is this: The identity of the antichrist will not be verbally revealed before he becomes visible, before he is seen with the naked eye; that is definitely not what Paul meant. In fact, it already has been proven exactly what Paul truly meant, but for the record, he absolutely does not mean that the identity of the antichrist will not be verbally revealed before he is seen; and this fact is actually very important to me, because if Paul meant that, then this book would be meaningless. So, that is why it's super important to fully and correctly understand what Paul is actually saying. Therefore, since Paul does not mean – at all -- that the identity of the antichrist will not be verbally revealed before he is seen, then it leaves only one other possibility, and that one and only possibility is that the identity of the antichrist either has already been revealed or will be revealed. Obviously, after coming this far in this very book, you know which choice is the truth, right?. No, don't make any mistake about it: The truth of the matter is that the identity of the antichrist has, indeed, *already been* verbally revealed, and that ought not to surprise you. Why? Oh, that's simple. So, the exact identity of the antichrist was already verbally revealed, right? Didn't the Lord Jesus already verbally reveal the identity of the antichrist when He was on that old rugged cross? Didn't He even say someone's actual name, a name absolutely not linked *in any which way or form* to His Father? Was not that name, the name Jesus exclusively uttered, "Eli?" Didn't He even say that very name twice? Isn't that *exactly* who the Lord Jesus was speaking to when He:

"...cried in a loud voice, saying, ELI, ELI LAMA SABACHTHANI?"

Yes! Yes, it was that name! It was the name, "Eli!" So, as a matter of indisputable fact, the identity of the antichrist – "...ELI, ELI..." – *has already been* correctly and verbally revealed. It sure has! It was correctly and verbally revealed when Jesus publicly and positively identified Eli as the antichrist, and the Lord did this when He literally spoke Eli's very name, saying it twice, in fact, and by calling out to him for all to hear – hence, "...ELI, ELI..."

Well, guess what? Believe it or not, there happens to be another way that Eli the Antichrist has already been verbally revealed. Yep, there sure is, and the proof is right here:

> "And that no man might buy or sell,
> Save he that had the mark, or the
> Name of the beast, or the number
> Of his name. Here is wisdom. Let
> Him that have understanding count
> The number of the beast: for it is a
> Number of a man; and his number
> Is Six hundred threescore and six."
> Revelation 13: 17-18

Whoa! Did you see that? Did you see that covered, hidden truth the Lord had the Apostle John write? Did you? It's right there in that very last sentence, and it's no doubt very important. It reads, "…and his number is Six hundred threescore and six." Whoa! I say, "Whoa!" Well, I now have a couple questions that I would like to ask: How many numbers are in "…Six hundred threescore and six?" Yeah, that's right. Three numbers is the correct answer. Ok, now, check this out: How many letters are in Eli's name? Bingo! Yeah, that's right. There are three letters in Eli's name, and three letters in "…Six hundred threescore and six." Now, why is that significant? I'll tell you why! It's significant because not only does it, once again, unquestionably prove that what Paul is not saying – the identity of the antichrist will not be verbally revealed before he is actually seen by the people on earth – is really not what he is saying, but it further proves even the more that Eli actually is 100%, without question the antichrist. How? Well, clearly when John was writing down and giving the whole world that awesome clue of 666, he did it obviously with Eli's name in mind to simply make the point that the antichrist's name will consist of three letters. And you know what else John did? Well, are you aware that the number six is a reference to man? Ok, so, basically, this is what John meant when he said "…Six hundred threescore and six:" Since Eli is a man, that is why the number six is being used; and it is used three times. Why? It is being used three times because John is telling us that the antichrist's name consists of exactly three letters – that's why. John basically covered up Eli's name with three sixes all because Eli is a man, and the number six is man's number; that's basically what happened. And for the record, who has exactly three letters in their name? Oh, I didn't hear you! Who does? That's right! Eli! Eli has exactly three letters in his name! So, the point is this: What we have here with the 666 verse, is that since Eli was already verbally revealed before he is actually *seen,* then Paul, as a matter of fact, really did mean that apokalupto, the Greek word for "revealed" in the scriptures truly does precisely mean that – that Eli will be verbally revealed before he is actually seen – hence, "…ELI, ELI…"

Lastly, if what the apostle Paul is not saying (or did not mean) was true, then Eli would not have been verbally revealed as the antichrist by Jesus, *and* John would not have verbally revealed him through the means of the 666 verse.

Alright, have you ever heard of the saying, "The Old Testament is the New Testament concealed, and the New

Testament is the Old Testament revealed?" Well, if you haven't, please allow me to be the first to tell you that it is utterly amazing! It really is, but, personally, I love it, because of how true it is. Yes, it is spot on, let me tell you. Basically, what it means is that both testaments, the New and the Old, speak of the same, truthful realities, but in the Old Testament those truthful realities are concealed, hidden away while in the New Testament, they are actually revealed. Neat, huh? What I'd like to do now is go ahead and give you some actual instances of this truly amazing saying. For starters, I'll start with two, general realities from God's word to serve as scriptural references, but afterwards, I'll only give examples of this amazing saying relating to the Ellic truths that are found exclusively in this book. With that said, here, now is that awesome saying in action:

- The Lord Jesus is concealed as the Lamb of God in the Old Testament (Genesis 22: 8) but is revealed in the New Testament (John 1: 29).
- The Lord Jesus is concealed as the Bread of Life in the Old Testament (Exodus 16: 15) but is revealed in the New Testament (John 6: 35).

- Eli is concealed in the Old Testament as the unredeemed ass (Exodus 13: 13) but is revealed in the New Testament (Revelation 13: 3).

- God, the Father's presence (the "…rod of God…") being with the Lord Jesus while on the cross is concealed in the Old Testament (Exodus 17: 9) but is revealed in the New Testament (Matthew 27: 46); this was done by the Lord Jesus publicly and exclusively identifying *Eli* as the one who is the antichrist – hence, "…ELI, ELI…"

- Eli is concealed in the Old Testament as the antichrist (1 Samuel 2: 3) but is revealed in the New Testament (2 Thessalonians 2: 4; Revelation 13: 5)

- Eli's stroke is concealed in the Old Testament (1 Samuel 4:18) but is revealed in the New Testament (Revelation 13: 3).

- Eli is concealed in the Old Testament as the antichrist (1 Samuel 2: 3) but is revealed in the New Testament (Matthew 27: 46).

- Eli is again concealed in the Old Testament as the antichrist (Job 41) but is revealed in the New Testament (Revelation 13: 2).

- Eli even again is concealed in the Old Testament as the antichrist (Isaiah 14: 16) but is revealed in the New Testament (Matthew 27: 46).

- Eli is once more concealed in the Old Testament as the antichrist (Isaiah 27: 1) but is revealed in the New Testament (Revelation 13:2).
- Eli is concealed in the Old Testament as the Curse of the Levitical Priests (Isaiah 65: 15) but is revealed in the New Testament (Revelation 13:2).

Well, that's pretty much it for this chapter. I hope you enjoyed it, and now you know why I titled this book, "To take off the cover."

Final Thoughts

Well, it's certainly been a journey, a long and challenging one, I think. So many new and amazing revelations have been exclusively revealed in this God-ordained, Holy Ghost-inspired book and, without a doubt, I sincerely hope that finally discovering the true, biblical identity of the antichrist that can *only* be found in Eli, by the way, has been an enjoyable and unforgettable experience. I really do. I know that I can definitely say that I have thoroughly enjoyed writing this book. While it has been a very long process and certainly not an easy one, I do know that just being given the wonderful privilege of correctly identifying and personally revealing Eli as the antichrist has absolutely been way more than I could have ever dreamed of or asked. Obviously, all of my thanks, my appreciation, and my deep gratitude go directly to my Father in Heaven, my Lord and Savior, Jesus Christ, and my own personal Counselor, the Holy Ghost. Boy, where would I be without those three? Without Them, this book surely wouldn't have been possible; no, it certainly wouldn't. After all, it's only because of Them that Eli has been correctly identified as well as positively revealed as the antichrist. They, without question, are the Ones who wholeheartedly deserve all of the credit, all of the glory, and all of the recognition.

Ok, since this chapter is the very last one of this entire book, I feel that some final thoughts that I personally have on certain topics should definitely be presented. So, having said that, it should be quickly noted that these forthcoming, final thoughts are at times random ideas of mine and may or may not include scriptural, supporting references. Alright? Ok, with that said, here are my final thoughts:

I believe – God did not tell me this; this is a hunch of mine – that Eli will reveal himself out of the sky. I believe he will astonishingly reveal himself by literally emerging out of the clouds and from the sky. Why? Well, as you read earlier in this book, the scriptures tell us that he will declare to the whole world that he is "God." Well, everyone knows where the real God dwells, right? Yeah, the *real* God dwells up in the sky, up in Heaven, to be specific. Everyone knows that. So, since the real God really does dwell up in Heaven and through the sky, I wholeheartedly believe that when Eli finally shows up, revealing his lying and pompous self to all of the world, he will do so by literally flying in and through big, white clouds (Remember, he will be in spirit form not flesh.), thereby grabbing all of the attention, gasps, finger-pointing and wondrous gazes of the totally unsuspecting and shocked people. Yes, I do believe this will ultimately happen. The Lord Jesus, by the way, will return the same way. Oh, you don't believe me? Ok, well, here's the proof:

> "And then shall they see the Son of man
> [the Lord Jesus] coming in the clouds
> With great power and glory."
> Mark 13: 26

> "And then shall they see the Son of man
> Coming in a cloud with power and great
> Glory."
> Luke 21: 27

> "Behold, he [the Lord Jesus] cometh with
> Clouds; and every eye shall see him, and
> They also which pierced him."
> Revelation 1: 7

Now, I am fully aware of the fact that when the Apostle John saw Eli in the revelatory vision that was given to him by Jesus, John saw Eli come up out of the sea (Revelation 13: 1), but I must say that the *real* reason why Eli did come out of the sea is because in the marvelous eyes of God, the sea is absolutely seen as wicked and 100% not something that is good. Yes, this is true, and here, now, is the proof:

> "But the wicked are like the troubled
> Sea, when it cannot rest, whose waters
> Cast up mire and dirt. There is no peace,
> Saith my God, to the wicked."
> Isaiah 57: 20-21

> "Hast thou entered into the springs of
> The sea? Or hast thou walked in the
> Search of the depth? Have the gates
> Of death been opened unto thee? Or
> Hast thou seen the doors of the shadow
> Of death?"
> Job 38: 16-17

> "Dead things are formed from under the
> Waters, and the inhabitants thereof. Hell
> [Yes, Hell was just mentioned.] is naked

Before him [God], and destruction
["…abaddon;"[28] "…The angel of the
bottomless pit…" – Revelation 9: 11] hath
no covering."
Job 26: 5-6

"They shall bring thee down to the pit,
And thou shalt die the deaths of them
That are slain in the midst of the seas."
Ezekiel 28: 8

"…and though they be hid from my sight
In the bottom of the sea, thence will I
Command the serpent [Who you think
that is?], and he shall bite them."
Amos 9: 3

"He [God] will turn again, he will have
Compassion on us; he will subdue our
Iniquities; and thou wilt cast all their sins
Into the depths of the sea."
Micah 7: 19

---

[28] Ibid., 1

"And the sixth angel sounded, and I [John]
Heard a voice from the four horns of the
Golden altar which is before God, saying to
The sixth angel which had the trumpet,
Loose the four angels which are bound in
The great river Euphrates."
Revelation 9: 13-14

"And the second angel poured out his vial
Upon the sea; and it became as the blood
Of a dead man: and every living soul died
In the sea. And the third angel poured out
His vial upon the rivers and fountains of
Waters; and they became blood. And I
[John] heard the angel of the waters say,
Thou art righteous, O Lord, which art, and
Wast, and shall be, because thou hast judged
Thus. For they [the evil beings in the
Sea] have shed the blood of saints and
Prophets, and thou hast given them
Blood to drink, for they are worthy."
Revelation 16: 3-6

Plus, don't forget: Eli, himself, as Leviathan, the Curse of the Levitical Priests, is actually depicted in the sea, and he, without a doubt, *certainly* is evil; here's the proof:

> "Canst thou draw out Leviathan with an
> Hook? He maketh the deep to boil like a
> Pot: he maketh the sea like a pot of ointment.
> He maketh a path to shine after him; one
> Would think the deep to be hoary."
> Job 41: 1; 31-32

> "Thou didst divide the sea by thy strength:
> Thou brakest the heads of the dragons
> In the waters. Thou brakest the heads
> Of Leviathan in pieces, and gavest him
> To be meat to the people inhabiting the
> Wilderness."
> Psalm 74: 13-14

> "So is this great and wide sea, wherein are
> Things creeping innumerable, both small
> And great beasts. There go the ships:
> There is that leviathan, whom thou hast
> Made to play therein."
> Psalm 104: 25-26

> "In that day the Lord with his sore and
> Great and strong sword shall punish
> Leviathan the piercing serpent, even
> Leviathan that crooked serpent; and he
> Shall slay the dragon [Satan] that is in the
> sea."
> Isaiah 27: 1

See, God really does see the sea as evil and sinful, and that is why when it is all said and done, when God finally gets rid of the stupid and unredeemed ass and his evil cohort, there will never, no *never* be a sea again; that's right. You read that last statement correctly. The sea will definitely no longer exist, and here, now, is your last juicy tidbit:

> "And I [John] saw a new heaven and a
> New earth: for the first heaven and the
> First earth were passed away; and there
> Was no more sea."
> Revelation 21: 1

Now, I must say that if all of those truly incredible scriptures don't prove the overwhelming fact that God really does view the sea as evil, then I'm not sure what would. Also, it is very obvious that not only does God view the sea as being wicked but also what's inside. Yes, I did just say that, and on a personal note, that is why I do not like the ocean or go to the beaches.

At this time, I'd like to point out a very revealing fact; it is this: The Apostle John states that Eli will blaspheme "…them that dwell in heaven" (Revelation 13: 6). Any guesses why? Well, I'll be happy to tell you. The reason why is because those that dwell in Heaven and who he will be speaking to are the very people he knew when he was down on earth the first time – people no doubt like the Prophet Samuel and Samuel's mother, Hannah. So, that's why John says that Eli will be blaspheming "… those that dwell in heaven."

Well, with the conclusion of that last supporting reference, I, sadly, have no more final thoughts to share with you; but I do have something else to say, and it is this:

For any of you that do not know the Lord Jesus as your personal Savior, I'd first like to personally tell you that He loves you very much and more than you probably realize. I also want you to know that the reason why He sent His *only* Son to pay for your personal penalty of sin, and the reason why He deliberately had this book written, was because of His genuine love for you; that's also why He sent His Son down to earth. God loves you, Ok? He really does, and He doesn't want you to stay unredeemed and literally die in your sins. So, having said that, I want to extend a very special offer to you. I want to offer you the incredible and truly wonderful chance of actually getting redeemed and becoming God's child. Will you do that? Will you get redeemed? Will you simply choose to be God's child right now instead of Satan's? It's real simple; it really is. In fact, I've done it myself. I did it at the tender age of four. So, you certainly can do it too and even right now this very second. All you have to do is just simply ask God to forgive you of your sins, ask Him to be your personal God, and tell Him that you want His Son, the Lord Jesus Christ, to personally redeem you and be your Savior; that's it; that's all you have to do. It's that easy, and it can be done right now. Here, pray the following prayer to God right now:

> "Father, please forgive me of my sins. I want
> You to forgive me. I want you to
> Be my God. I want your Son, the Lord Jesus
> Christ, to redeem me and be my
> Personal Savior. Please, Father. Come into
> my life. Right now. In Jesus name,
> Amen."

"The secret things belong unto the Lord our God: but those things which are revealed belong unto us and to our children for ever..."
Deuteronomy 29: 29

ACKNOWLEDGEMENTS

- I'd like to thank Dr. Willmington for allowing me to include his insightful commentary on God's word.

- I'd like to personally salute Jimmy Swaggart's *"The Expositor's Study Bible."* Your bible is amazing, Mr. Swaggart.

- Bob and Sandy: Thank you so much for everything.

- Ma, I love you. I miss you. I did it.

BIBLIOGRAPHY

Taken from *THE NEW STRONG'S EXHAUSTIVE CONCORDANCE OF THE BIBLE* by Strong, James, LL.D., S.T.D. Copyright [1990] by [James Strong, LL.D., S.T.D.]. Used by permission of Thomas Nelson. www.thomasnelson.com

Swaggart, Jimmy. The Expositor's Study Bible. (Baton Rouge. Jimmy Swaggart.Ministries. 2010). www.jsm.org

Willmington, H.L. Willmington's Guide to the Bible. (Wheaton. Tyndale House Publishers, Inc. 1984). www.tyndale.com